The Political Economy of Biodiversity Policy Reform

OECD
BETTER POLICIES FOR BETTER LIVES

Please cite this publication as:
OECD (2017), *The Political Economy of Biodiversity Policy Reform*, OECD Publishing, Paris.
http://dx.doi.org/10.1787/9789264269545-en

ISBN 978-92-64-26952-1 (print)
ISBN 978-92-64-26954-5 (PDF)
ISBN 978-92-64-26955-2 (ePub)

Photo credits: © Shutterstock\Taiga.

Corrigenda to OECD publications may be found on line at: *www.oecd.org/about/publishing/corrigenda.htm*.

Preface

The sustainable management of ecosystems and biodiversity is vital both for economic development and human well-being. The need for more far-reaching and ambitious policies has been repeatedly called for under the Convention on Biological Diversity. More recently, the Sustainable Development Goals reiterated this imperative with dedicated goals for both marine and terrestrial ecosystems.

Despite some progress, current efforts are being overwhelmed by burgeoning global claims on natural goods and services to support economic activity. Yet ecosystem services provide the irreplaceable foundations for life on Earth. Biodiversity policies need to be more ambitious. Policies devised for sectors such as agriculture and fisheries have to start from the premise that their survival depends on healthy, functioning ecosystems. Policies that undermine – like environmentally harmful subsidies – *must* be reformed. The policy solutions needed to underwrite biodiversity are not neither novel nor particularly complex. It is their implementation that is lagging.

This report on *The Political Economy of Biodiversity Policy Reform* examines how governments have navigated the challenges of implementing reform. It highlights the types of barriers that are encountered along the way and how they can be overcome. The report brings together insights from the relevant literature on environmental policy reform and four new country case studies. The case studies examine pesticide taxes to address agricultural pollution, agricultural subsidy reform to better target biodiversity, tradable quotas to prevent collapse of fish stocks, and the establishment of conservation trust funds to provide sustainable financing for marine protected areas.

Policies designed to promote biodiversity will always be context-dependent. Institutions, actors and motives cannot easily be generalised. But the experience of past and on-going reforms provides proof that reform is, indeed, possible. And these reforms can provide powerful lessons that can increase the prospect of success of biodiversity reforms in other countries.

Simon Upton
Director, OECD Environment Directorate

Foreword

More ambitious policies for biodiversity conservation and sustainable use are necessary to stem the global decline in biodiversity. However, progress on scaling up biodiversity policies, and the reform of policies that are harmful to biodiversity, has not been as rapid or effective as needed. As countries strive to implement more ambitious and cost-effective biodiversity policies, policy makers often encounter a number of barriers. These may include concerns about potential competitiveness impacts or distributional issues, and the influence of vested interests or the political and social acceptability of reform. Greater insights are needed into how policy decisions are made, in whose interests and how reform is promoted or obstructed and why – in other words, understanding the political economy of biodiversity policy reform.

There is today a substantial and growing body of literature on the political economy of environmental policy, in particular on climate and energy policy. Previous OECD work in this area includes The Political Economy of Environmentally Related Taxes *(2006) and* Fisheries Policies Reform: National Experiences *(2011). Much less attention, however, has been paid to biodiversity relevant policy reform, a gap which this report contributes to addressing. This report draws on the literature on salient issues that arise in the context of environmental policy reform and highlights examples relevant to biodiversity. Four new case studies are then examined: the French tax on pesticides; agricultural subsidy reform in Switzerland; European Union payments to Mauritania and Guinea-Bissau to finance marine protected areas management via conservation trust funds; and individually transferable quotas for fisheries in Iceland. Each case study focusses on the drivers of reform, the types of obstacles encountered, key features of the policy reform, and the lessons learned from the reform experience. Insights from this report can serve as inspiration for reform efforts elsewhere, as countries seek to implement more ambitious and cost-effective policies to enhance biodiversity conservation and sustainable use.*

Acknowledgements

This report was prepared by Kathleen Dominique and Katia Karousakis of the OECD Environment Directorate. The contributions to the chapters are as follows: Chapters 1 and 4 have been authored by Kathleen Dominique and Katia Karousakis; Chapter 2 has been authored by Katia Karousakis and Naazia Ebrahim (formerly also at the OECD Environment Directorate); Chapter 3 has been authored by Kathleen Dominique; Fabien Quetier and Ariane Amin (BIOTOPE) authored Chapter 5; and Gunnar Haraldsson (Founder, Intellecon) authored Chapter 6.

The authors gratefully acknowledge the valuable insights obtained during various interviews conducted to enrich the case studies, namely:

- For the case study on the evolution of the tax on pesticides and the pesticide savings certificates in France (Chapter 3): Philippe Puydarrieux, Francois-Xavier Pourquier, Valerie To, Jérémy Devaux, Lucile Gauchet, Emilie Gallouet, Xavier Jardi and Doris Nicklaus from the French Ministry of Environment, Energy and the Sea; Frédéric Vey and Laurent Jacquiau from the Ministry of Agriculture, Food and Forestry; Dominique Potier, Deputy of Meurthe et Moselle, National Assembly; Dominique Bureau, Chair of the Green Economy Committee; Nelly Le Corre, Department of economics and sustainable development, Fédération nationale des syndicats d'exploitants agricoles (FNSEA); Vincent Magdelaine, Director, Coop de France. In addition, further comments were obtained via correspondence with Guillaume Sainteny, former Chair of the Commission on Public Incentives Harmful to Biodiversity and Olivier Bommelaer, former Counsellor at the permanent delegation of France to the OECD.
- For the case study on the reform of the system of direct payments to agriculture in Switzerland (Chapter 4): Swiss Federal Office of the Environment: Hans Gujer and Gabriella Blatter; Swiss Federal Office of Agriculture: Jérôme Frei and Judith Ladner Callipari; Kathrin Bertschy, Member of Parliament; Marcel Liner, ProNatura; Werner Müller, Birdlife International; and Christophe Dietler, Agrarallianz.
- For the case study on EU Payments to Mauritania and Guinea-Bissau for MPA conservation under the Fisheries Partnership Agreements (Chapter 5): Arnaud Appriou, European External Action Service delegation in Mauritania; Celestina Bastos, European External Action Service delegation in Guinea-Bissau; Moussa Beddiyouh, Agence Française de Développement Mauritania; Guillaume Chiron, Agence Française de Développement; Sylvie Goyet, Fondation Internationale du Banc d'Arguin, Ahmed Lefghih, BACoMaB Trust Fund; Thierry Renaud, MAVA Foundation; Tanya Yudelman, consultant to the World Bank.

Special thanks are due to Xavier Jardi and Philippe Puydarrieux (French Ministry of Environment, Energy and the Sea) for their help in co-ordinating the interviews related to the French case study, as well as to Gabriella Blatter, Andreas Hauser and Gabriella Silvestri (Swiss Federal Office of the Environment) and Jérôme Frei (Swiss Federal Office of Agriculture) for their assistance with the Swiss case study.

In addition, the authors benefitted from valuable comments provided by delegates of the OECD Working Party on Biodiversity, Water and Ecosystems (WPBWE) as well as OECD colleagues, including: Nils Axel Braathen, Bob Diderich, Guillaume Guère, Julien Hardelin, Richard Sigman and Frédérique Zegel (on the French case study); Václav Vojtech and Jussi Lankowski (on the Swiss case study); Roger Martini and James Innes (on the Icelandic case study) as well as Simon Buckle. Angèle N'zinga provided valuable administrative support.

Finally, financial contributions from Switzerland to support this project are also gratefully acknowledged.

Table of contents

Tables

Figures

Acronyms

AP 2014-17	Swiss Agricultural Policy 2014-17
BAFU	Swiss Federal Office for the Environment (*Das Bundesamt für Umwelt*)
BLW	Swiss Federal Office for Agriculture (*Bundesamt für Land-wirtschaft*)
BOD	Biochemical oxygen demand
CAP	EU Common Agricultural Policy
CBD	The United Nation's Convention on Biological Diversity
CEPPs	Pesticide saving certificates, France (*Certificats d'économie de produits phytosanitaires*)
CFP	European Union's Common Fisheries Policy
CTF	Conservation trust fund
CVP	Christian Democratic People's Party of Switzerland
ECAs	Ecological compensation areas (in Switzerland)
EEZ	Exclusive economic zone
EU	European Union
EUFS	Environmental User Fee System
FDP	Free Democratic Party of Switzerland
FIBA	International Foundation of the Banc d'Arguin (*Fondation Internationale du Banc d'Arguin*)
FNSEA	National Federation of Agricultural Trade Unions, France (*Fédération Nationale des Syndicats d'Exploitants d'Agricoles*)
FOAG	Swiss Federal Office of Agriculture
FOEN	Swiss Federal Office for the Environment
FPAs	European Union Fisheries Partnership Agreements
GATT	General Agreement on Trade and Tariffs
GDP	Gross domestic product
GEF	Global Environment Facility
INRA	French National Institute for Agricultural Research (*L'Institut National de la Recherche Agronomique*)
ITQs	Individually transferable quotas
IUCN	International Union for the Conservation of Nature
LAAF	Law on the Future of Agriculture and Forestry, France (*Loi d'Avenir Agricole et Forestiere*)
LEMA	Law on Water and Aquatic Environments, France (*Loi sur l'eau et les milieux aquatiques*)
MAAF	French Ministry of Agriculture, Food and Forest
MEDDE	French Ministry of Ecology and Sustainable Development
MENR	Icelandic Ministry of Environment and Natural Resources
MPA	Marine protected area

NBS	National Biodiversity Strategy
NGO	Non-governmental organisation
NODU	Number of Unit Doses
OECD	Organisation for Economic Co-operation and Development
PEP	Proof of ecological performance
PES	Payments for ecosystem services
PNBA	Banc d'Arguin National Park of Mauritania
PSE	Producer Support Estimate
QMS	New Zealand's Individually Tradable Quota Management System
RFMOs	Regional fishery management organisations
SP	The Social Democratic Party of Switzerland
SVP	The Swiss People's Party
TAC	Total allowable catch
TGAP	General tax on polluting activities, France (*Taxe générale sur les activités polluantes*)
UAA	Utilised Agriculture Area
UNCLOS	United Nations Convention on the Law of the Sea
VAT	Value added tax
WTO	World Trade Organisation

Executive summary

The need for more widespread and ambitious policy instruments for biodiversity conservation and sustainable use, including the reform of incentives that are harmful to biodiversity, is widely acknowledged. Progress, however, has not been as rapid and effective as needed. Global biodiversity trends continue to decline and the *OECD Environmental Outlook to 2050* projects this to continue under a business-as-usual scenario (OECD, 2012). Loss of biodiversity and associated ecosystems in turn, results in adverse and costly impacts on human health, well-being and economic growth.

As countries strive to implement more ambitious and cost-effective policies to enhance biodiversity conservation and sustainable use, a key question is why some policy reforms relating to biodiversity have been successful, while others have not. Though there is a growing body of literature on the political economy of environmental policy reform, much less attention has been devoted to biodiversity, or biodiversity relevant, policy reform. Taking a political economy perspective on biodiversity related policy reform i.e. the political constraints that condition the timing, speed and sequencing of reform, can shed light on this, and consequently, help to provide insight on how barriers to reform can be addressed.

This report aims to contribute in this regard. It summarises the salient political economy issues that arise in environmental policy reform more broadly, and highlights cases where these have arisen in the context of biodiversity relevant policy reform. Four new case studies follow, highlighting insights and lessons that emerge from each experience. The case studies are: the French tax on pesticides; agricultural subsidy reform in Switzerland; European Union (EU) payments to Mauritania and Guinea-Bissau to finance marine protected areas management via conservation trust funds as part of Fisheries Partnership Agreements; and individually transferable quotas (ITQs) for fisheries in Iceland. Each of these case studies focusses on the policy context in which the reform was undertaken; the drivers of reform and the types of obstacles that have been encountered; key features of the policy reform and the impacts on various sectors; and the lessons learned from the reform experiences, including insights on how obstacles were addressed.

Drawing on the literature and the experiences from the case studies examined here, the insights and lessons learned on overcoming obstacles to more effective biodiversity policy reform are summarised below.

- Salient issues that arise in the political economy of environmental policy are competitiveness concerns, impacts on income distribution, vested interests, and the political acceptability of reform. These issues also resonate strongly in the biodiversity related policy reforms examined in this report.
- Potential adverse impacts on competitiveness can act both as a driver and as a barrier to reform. In the case of Iceland, the looming threat of an economic crisis due to the

impending fisheries collapse led to a rapid and sweeping reform of domestic fisheries policy. Barring an economic crisis however, stakeholders have most often used potentially adverse impacts on competitiveness as an argument for slower and more piecemeal policy reform. This is illustrated in the case of France. Revenue-recycling of the tax on pesticides was one approach that helped to mitigate these concerns.

- Concerns regarding the impacts of policy reform on income distribution have also been important in the case studies on France, Switzerland, and Iceland. In Iceland, discontent with the way the initial free allocation of fisheries quotas had led to a distinct set of "winners" was an important driver of more recent policy reforms, which introduced a resource rent tax on fishery quotas to more broadly share the benefits from a common property resource. In Switzerland, transition payments were used to minimise negative impacts on farmers who would no longer receive payments per head of cattle.
- Developing a robust evidence base can help to build support for policy reform. Such an evidence base has helped French authorities resist pressure from vested interests. The identification of costs and benefits of reform amongst various stakeholders and over time can help to identify possible allies in the case for reform, as well as how to better target compensational and transitional measures as illustrated in the Swiss case. Moreover, communicating evidence to the general public can enhance the political acceptability of the reform.
- In addition to finding ways to design policies and build support for reform so as to reduce the (real or perceived) obstacles, the case studies presented here also point to the need to be ready to act quickly to take advantage of windows of opportunity that are often outside the influence of domestic policy-makers. This can include forming coalitions, either explicitly or behind-the-scenes, with other interest groups who may share the same desired outcomes, though their own motivations may not be driven by concerns for biodiversity or the environment more broadly. This is shown in the case of Switzerland, where economic and environmental interests aligned to support reform.
- It is also important to ensure that reforms are sustained over time. Vested interests, for example, do not simply disintegrate once a policy reform has been enacted – political priorities can shift and governments can change. Similarly, when there is high turn-over of leadership or staff in key institutions, a void may be created when champions or experts move on, resulting in existing policies becoming vulnerable to back-tracking. These challenges have arisen in the case studies on the conservation trust funds in Mauritania and Guinea-Bissau and in the agricultural policy reform in Switzerland. Continuous training, awareness raising, and provision of evidence-based results can help to maintain successful reforms over time.
- Finally, and similar to findings on environmental and fishery policy reform more broadly, this report re-iterates that there is no "one size fits all" approach to biodiversity relevant policy reform. Strategies to overcome barriers to biodiversity related reforms need to be tailored to the specific context, institutional and political setting of a given country. For example, while broad stakeholder engagement was an important factor in driving incremental policy reform in the French and Swiss case, the lack of broad stakeholder engagement is credited with facilitating the speed with which fisheries reforms in Iceland was undertaken, after which a series of piecemeal reforms were required to address persistent stakeholder concerns.

Chapter 1

The political economy of biodiversity policy reform: Lessons learned

This chapter draws out the main themes related to the political economy of biodiversity policy reform, derived from the analysis of the case studies in this report. It summarises the lessons learned from the case studies and provides a number of insights on overcoming obstacles to effective biodiversity policy reform.

1.1. The need for more ambitious biodiversity policy reform

The need for more widespread and ambitious policy instruments for biodiversity conservation and sustainable use, including the reform of incentives that are harmful to biodiversity, is widely acknowledged. Progress, however, has not been as rapid and effective as needed and global biodiversity trends continue to decline (Butchart et al., 2010). The OECD *Environmental Outlook to 2050* projects continued declines under a business-as-usual scenario (OECD, 2012). Loss of biodiversity and ecosystems results in adverse and costly impacts on human health, well-being and economic growth. At the international level, Parties to the Convention on Biological Diversity (CBD) have committed to achieving the 2011-20 Aichi Biodiversity Targets, many of which are also echoed in the more recent Sustainable Development Goals. As the 4th *Global Biodiversity Outlook* emphasises,[1] more concerted policy efforts are needed to attain these goals (CBD, 2014).

Such calls for action are not, by any means, new.[2] However, Aichi Biodiversity Target 3, introduced under the Strategic Plan for Biodiversity under the CBD in 2010, contains specific language on the need to reform harmful incentives and apply positive incentives.[3] This has helped to renew the political impetus for action and, in 2012, led to a call to consider modalities and milestones for its operationalisation. As countries strive to implement more ambitious and cost-effective policies to enhance the conservation and sustainable use of biodiversity, additional insights are needed as to why some biodiversity related policy reforms have made progress, while others have not.

Insights on the barriers to biodiversity related reform and how they can be overcome can be drawn from examining the political economy of reform – i.e. how decisions are made, in whose interests and how reform is promoted or obstructed and why (OECD, 2011a). Decision text of CBD COP 12 highlights the need for this type of work by inviting Parties to submit information on *practical experiences in the implementation of biodiversity related positive incentives and lessons learned in applying options for overcoming obstacles encountered in implementing policies for addressing harmful incentives* (Decision XII/L.32, para 23).

While there is a growing body of literature on the political economy of environmental policy in general (e.g. IMF, 2013; Elkins and Salmons, 2010; Sutinen, 2008; World Bank, 2008; OECD, 2006; Felder and Schleiniger, 2002), much less attention has been devoted to biodiversity related policy reforms. Similarly, while there is literature on the political economy of agricultural reform and fisheries reform (e.g., OECD, 2011b; OECD 2011c; Swinnen, 2010; De Gorter and Swinnen, 2002), both sectors that are relevant for biodiversity, these studies do not necessarily focus on the biodiversity aspects of reform. This report aims to address this gap by drawing lessons learned from several case studies on biodiversity related policy reforms.

Some of the salient issues that arise in the political economy of environmental policy include competitiveness issues, distributional implications, vested interests, and political acceptability. These issues are also relevant for the four biodiversity relevant policy reforms examined in this report. The case studies examined are: the French tax on pesticides; the reform of agricultural support in Switzerland; European Union (EU) payments to Mauritania and Guinea-Bissau to finance marine protected areas via conservation trust funds as part of Fisheries Partnership Agreements; and individually transferable quotas (ITQs) and the resource rent tax for fisheries in Iceland.

1.2. Insights on overcoming obstacles to effective biodiversity policy reform

The case studies provide a number of insights on overcoming obstacles to effective biodiversity related reforms. While the policy and institutional settings, actors and motives driving reforms combine in unique ways in each context, learning from the experience of past and on-going reforms can help to illuminate wider lessons that can increase the prospect of success of biodiversity related reforms in other countries. This section draws out the main themes that have emerged across the case studies and the lessons learned.

Stand ready to seize opportunities to advance biodiversity related reforms: from crisis to public concern

Each of the case studies reveals a distinct pattern of reform drivers, which illustrates the diversity of opportunities to advance biodiversity related reforms. The case studies point to the need to be ready to act quickly when presented with windows of opportunity that may be outside the influence of domestic policy-makers and unrelated to environmental concerns. For example, Iceland provides a clear example of a common theme in the political economy of reform: the crisis as catalyst. The major reform of Icelandic fishery policy was driven by an urgent need to prevent the imminent collapse of an economically important industry. While biodiversity was not an explicit aim of the reform, safeguarding biodiversity was a positive by-product of the reform, which put the fisheries sector on a more sustainable footing.

In Switzerland, several factors came together to provide an auspicious environment for the reform of agricultural support. The composition of the Parliament in 2013 was particularly conducive to approving the reform that had been in preparation over the preceding years. The Parliamentary elections in 2011 saw the Green Liberal Party successfully ride the wave of anti-nuclear sentiment in the aftermath of the environmental disaster at Japan's Fukushima plant in March of that year (The Guardian, 2011). The current Parliament is more conservative, with greater representation of one of the political parties that had opposed the reform. It is questionable whether the reform of the direct payments system to agriculture to better target public goods, including biodiversity benefits, would have been approved given the political composition of the current Parliament. Further, the reform was developed under the leadership of the then Director of the Federal Office of Agriculture (FOAG) who is credited with being an important influence on driving reform.

For France, growing public concern about the potential risks of pesticide use to human health and the environment has become an increasingly important reform driver, opening opportunities for stronger policy action. While the influence of public pressure is more difficult to trace in earlier stages of the reform, it is clear is that public opinion, as expressed through market choices (via growing demand for organic products and willingness to pay a premium for such products) is increasingly prominent. Heightened media attention, campaigns by NGOs, and swelling public pressure have given momentum to further action on specific types of pesticides. A notable example is the French Parliament's ratification in June 2016 of a ban on neonicotinoids (insecticides with harmful impacts on bee populations) starting in 2018. Strong public pressure and concerted engagement from the Minister of Ecology helped to push for policy action on this issue.

Build alliances between economic and environmental interests

Several of the case studies illustrate how economic and environmental interests can be aligned to build support for biodiversity related reform. In the cases of Iceland and Switzerland, biodiversity concerns were not an explicit objective of reforms or only a secondary factor. Building alliances between economic and environmental interests can advance reforms beneficial for biodiversity in instances where a more narrow focus on only "green" issues might fail. This can include forming coalitions, either explicitly or behind-the-scenes, with other interest groups who may share the same desired outcomes, though their motivations may not at all be driven by concerns for biodiversity or the environment more broadly. Making a clear link showing how greater provision of ecosystem services can generate economic benefits is also a useful strategy, which was important in the case of Mauritania and Guinea-Bissau.

In Switzerland, arguably, the main impetus for the change in agricultural policy was support for market-oriented reforms to encourage free trade and bring the direct payments system more closely in alignment with World Trade Organisation's (WTO) "Green Box" criteria.[4] Building a coalition among market-oriented interests promoting trade liberalisation and environmental interests was particularly crucial for advancing the reform. Concerns for biodiversity and ecosystems were important as well, but a secondary factor. Active lobbying by environmental NGOs using both economic and environmental arguments helped to win support in Parliament.

In the case of Mauritania and Guinea-Bissau, concerted lobbying efforts by environmental NGOs to clearly link the economic benefits to fisheries of well-functioning ecosystem services helped to gain financing for conservation trust funds for marine protected areas (MPAs). A well-established and credible "broker", the environmental NGO the International Foundation of the Banc d'Arguin (*Fondation Internationale du Banc d'Arguin*, FIBA), played a key role in establishing a shared understanding of the benefits that MPAs bring to the fishing sector and the benefits trust funds bring to marine conservation. This required concerted lobbying in the co-ordination of those involved in country, in the European Union, and in the broader donor community. In Guinea-Bissau, another environmental NGO, the International Union for the Conservation of Nature (IUCN), also played an important role by laying the ground work for broader institutional change concerning conservation.

Devise targeted measures to address potential impacts on competitiveness and income distribution

The examples of France, Iceland and Switzerland illustrate the importance of minimising costs of reform on targeted sectors and stakeholders as a means to overcome potential opposition to reform. The cases show how the distribution of costs and benefits (real or perceived) can be fundamental in defining the ambition and pace of reforms, policy choice and design. Recycling the revenue from environmentally related taxes or putting into place transitional measures can help to minimise the cost to affected sectors. Other economic instruments can be used to address distributional concerns, such as resource rent taxes, to more widely share the benefits of harvesting common property resources.

In the case of France, as Europe's leading agricultural producer, limiting the potential costs to the agricultural sector of policies to reduce pesticide use has been a prerequisite to advancing reform. Recycling the revenue from the tax on diffuse pollution to mainly benefit farmers helped to gain the political acceptability of the tax and subsequent increases in the tax rate and the expansion of the tax-base. This revenue recycling mechanism was also a critical factor that supported maintaining the ambitious reduction targets under the Ecophyto Plan II, when the results of the previous plan, Ecophyto I, fell well short of targets to reduce pesticide use by 50%. Moreover, the removal of the reduced value-added tax (VAT) rate on pesticides did not affect production costs for most farmers, as they benefit from a simplified VAT scheme. This, undoubtedly, contributed to the acceptance of the removal of this environmentally-harmful subsidy, one of the very few recommendations from the 2011 national study on public subsidies harmful to biodiversity (Sainteny, 2011) that was successfully implemented.

Also in the case of France, concerns about potential negative impacts on competitiveness on the agricultural sector have been sufficient to limit the increases in the rate of the tax on diffuse pollution to modest levels, far below those that could have a strong incentive impact on pesticide use. Although, recognising that moderate pesticide use reduction need not be at odds with the competitivity of agricultural firms may provide a powerful means to overcome this persistent barrier to more ambitious action. As argued by Potier (2014), the experience of farmers already engaged in reducing pesticide use – from the pioneers of sustainable agriculture to the champions of precision agriculture – demonstrates that such systems can deliver economic, environmental and social benefits, without reducing agricultural production.

In Iceland, the reform has been a clear success measured in economic efficiency and as a way of drastically reducing fishing effort to safeguard the sustainability of the fish stocks. However, there were distinct winners and losers which led to subsequent reforms to meet certain economic and political demands. Introducing a property rights based system, such as ITQs, leads to changes that benefit some more than others, especially when fishing rights are freely transferable. Much of the discontent over the years following the reform has been due to the initial free allocation of the quotas to existing fishers based on their recent catch levels at the time. This approach of initially grandfathering fishing rights is very common for property rights based systems because it is often the easiest approach from a political perspective and it can have positive efficiency advantages compared to some other means of distribution. However, even more than three decades later, this is considered by some people in and outside of the industry to have been an unjust way of disbursing rights to harvest a commonly owned resource. People who live in fishing regions where quotas are sold or leased are often left with few other employment opportunities and can experience economic and social hardships. Although the quota owners receive payment for their quotas, others that depended on the fishing activity for their livelihood, directly or indirectly, do not receive such payments.

The resource rent tax introduced in 2012 sought to remedy some of the distributional issues related to the initial free allocation of quotas. The aim is to ensure that the general public in Iceland receives benefits from the commonly owned fish resources. Although it is undeniable that the Icelandic economy has benefitted greatly from a more efficient fishing industry, the ITQ system generates resource rents to companies in the industry and claims have been made that these resource rents should accrue to a greater extent to the general public. While the resource rent tax has provided increased revenues to the state, there is still discussion about the appropriate level of the tax and whether other methods to collect the resource rent, such as auctioning, would be preferred.

For Switzerland, advancing reforms to better target agricultural support required devising politically and socially acceptable compromises in the reform package. The

Agricultural Policy 2014-17 (AP 2014-17) included an important compromise to balance interests, which facilitated its approval by Parliament. This consisted of maintaining the overall level of budgetary support for agriculture (in fact, the overall level increased slightly) while re-distributing that support across the new categories of payments (including biodiversity payments). Through this major compromise, the agricultural sector as a whole receives slightly increased budgetary payments over the 2014-17 period, while the level of direct payments either increases or decreases for various groups of farmers. For example, alpine farmers in particular benefitted from more payments for extensive production and biodiversity payments under the new system. At the same time, farmers no longer receive payments per head of cattle, affecting in particular, those with intensive cattle operations in the lowland region of the country.

In addition, transition payments were included in the reform package to minimise negative impacts on farmers. The most contentious and hotly debated change was the removal of payments per head of cattle. These payments constituted an important fraction of total payments for certain farmers and it was this element of the reform where the ultimate "losers" were clearly identifiable. Transition payments were provided to help offset expected income losses to farmers no longer receiving the payments per head of cattle. In addition, the animal related payments under the previous system were largely shifted to the category of food security payments.

Use a robust evidence base to build support for reform and provide resistance to pressure from vested interests

A robust scientific and economic evidence base can be a valuable tool in the arsenal of governments seeking to advance policy reforms. Such an evidence base can help to clearly identify the benefits and beneficiaries of reform, make the case for change and provide means to resist pressure from vested interests. In the case of Switzerland, environmental NGOs played a key role as part of their lobbying efforts to disseminate information about expected benefits of reforms to specialised agricultural groups, such as alpine farmers, which benefitted from more payments for extensive production and biodiversity payments under the new system. This helped to encouraged their engagement to support the reform process.

In the case of France, a robust evidence base supported by scientific research has been critical for the government to stand firm against lobbying pressure in the context of the recent introduction of the pesticides savings certificates. Ensuring a robust, scientifically supported link between the approved actions under these newly established pesticide savings certificates and actual reductions in pesticide use is essential for the success of the scheme. Yet, there has been limited economic evaluation of the costs of negative externalities from pesticide use in France. Incomplete information on total environmental and health costs to society of pesticide use impedes a more thorough cost-benefit analysis of pesticide use and better understanding of the distribution of costs and benefits to society. Such information could reinforce support by both policy makers and the public for reform. At the same time, incomplete information should not be used as a reason to delay action.

Encourage stakeholder engagement to build broad and durable support for reform

The cases of France, Switzerland and Iceland reveal distinct approaches to stakeholder engagement, with differing outcomes. In France and Switzerland stakeholder engagement has been very broad and intensive. This has meant that reforms have been incremental, proceeding at a slow pace, but generally moving in a positive direction. Also, in France, this approach to stakeholder engagement has been credited with helping to set ambitious targets in terms of pesticide use reduction. In contrast, limited stakeholder engagement likely contributed to the speedy adoption of more drastic reforms to establish the comprehensive ITQ system in Iceland.

In France, broad stakeholder engagement inspired by the "Grenelle model" along with the close co-operation between the Ministries of Environment and Agriculture, has been key to overcoming resistance of vested interest to reforms. Greater representativeness of stakeholders has had a positive influence on policy reforms in this case, as it has encouraged the engagement of a number of smaller, innovative pioneers who are helping to advance the agro-ecology agenda. Although this time-consuming and resource-intensive consultation process means that progress has been rather slow and modest, it is generally moving in a positive direction. However, the Grenelle approach of broad engagement does not eliminate the diversity of opinions and interests. While it is unlikely that French would have adopted such ambitious targets to reduce pesticide use in the absence of Grenelle, achieving these objectives still requires steady political will.

For Switzerland, the unique political system, with elements of direct democracy, means that reforms involve many stakeholders and extensive consultations. As a result, agreeing policy reforms and implementing them is a lengthy, but well-structured process. In the case of the reform of the direct payments system, broad stakeholder consultation helped to involve not only major lobbying groups including environmental NGOs, economics institutions, like economiesuisse, and the Farmers' Union, but also engaged smaller agricultural groups, including organic farmers associations and farmers located in alpine areas, who were well-positioned to benefit from the reform. Similar to the case of France, this greater representativeness allowed for the inclusion of smaller groups, which could better express the heterogeneous interests of the agricultural sector. At the same time, there is a strong public consensus about the multi-functional purpose of agriculture in the adoption of Article 104, which was adopted by popular vote.

In Iceland, the major reform to establish the ITQ system was led mainly by government authorities, including scientists. Some industry stakeholders, such as fishers and people whose livelihood depended to a great extent on the fishing (such as people in the processing industry and people living in rural areas dependent on fishing) were not explicitly engaged in the reform and the implementation of the ITQ system. Limited initial stakeholder engagement may have led to piecemeal amendments to the system over time to respond to specific stakeholder demands. For example, regional quotas were put in place to support communities where fishing is an economic mainstay, with variable results. Exemptions from the ITQ system were afforded for small vessels with the aim to protect rural employment, but undermined the sustainability of the system. In addition, a coastal fisheries system was devised to accommodate new entrants with small vessels, but the efficiency of the system is questionable.

If these stakeholders had been engaged in the reform process early on, a different system may have emerged than the ITQ system that was eventually adopted. At the same time, it may be argued that such sweeping reforms would have been difficult to implement as quickly, if the process had included the participation of all the different stakeholders. Including every possible stakeholder group would have taken time and resulted in a political debate at every step of the process. Generally, stakeholder engagement can help secure the broad support and durability of reforms. Where governments need to act quickly to avert a crisis, a balance needs to be struck to provide opportunities for stakeholder engagement, without unduly delaying the reform process.

Consolidate gains to ensure that reforms are sustained over time

The cases reviewed in this report also attest to the importance of ensuring that reforms are sustained over time, a theme raised in the broader political economy literature. Vested interests, for example, do not simply disintegrate once a policy reform has been enacted. As the influence of political parties changes as a result of election cycles, and new coalitions emerge, political priorities can shift. Similarly, when there is high turn-over of leadership and staff in key institutions, a void may be created when champions or experts move on, resulting in existing policies becoming vulnerable to back-tracking. These challenges have arisen in the case study on Mauritania and Guinea-Bissau where resources are scarce and financing dedicated to the endowment competes with short term sectoral priorities. Continuous training of staff, awareness raising, provision of evidence-based results, and active lobbying can help to maintain successful reforms over time. Furthermore, agreements with a firm legal basis will be more enduring that those based on an informal understanding, which can be contested and altered once leadership changes.

In the case of Mauritania, wavering political support threatens the long-term stability of the conservation trust fund. Early momentum to establish financing arrangements for conservation trust funds has dissipated somewhat, as government priorities have shifted away from conservation and competition for scarce financial resources for short term sectorial priorities threatens the continued capitalisation of the funds. The opportunity cost of allocating finance to the conservation trust funds (rather than to more immediate needs) is felt acutely by the government, while the benefits of such arrangements (by promoting more sustainable fisheries) accrue to a wide range of actors (fishers, tourists) over a longer period of time and in a more diffuse way. Further, the recent context of low interest rates challenges the rationale for placing funds in an endowment.

The transitory nature of the arrangement could also jeopardise long term commitments, as Fisheries Partnership Agreements (FPAs) and protocols are renegotiated on a regular basis as are government budgets. Paradoxically, such uncertainties in the continued commitment of governments are one of the main justifications for establishing conservation trust funds in the first place. One option to address this is would be for the EU to directly finance the trust funds to ensure its own goals (and financial management rules) under the Common Fisheries Policy are met. Moreover, to maintain local support, conservation trust funds must also rapidly demonstrate their potential as actual grant-makers. Associating revolving and sinking funds to endowments would help mitigate this perceived "taking-away" of scarce and valuable resources from short-term needs.

Securing progress towards conservation goals requires funding mechanisms that are financially and institutionally sustainable, such as conservation trust funds. However, a strong and stable institutional framework underpinning the financial arrangement that goes beyond a handshake agreement is equally important. In Mauritania, the capitalisation of the endowment was based on an informal understanding and quickly challenged after leadership changes in key institutions putting at risk the partnership between the trust fund and the protected area authorities. A possible solution could be to increase the independence of the trust fund making it an autonomous player, which can defend its role and interests, and establish a national constituency.

In the case of Switzerland, not long after the reform of the AP 2014-17 was voted by Parliament, the Farmers' Union launched a call for a popular initiative proposing a change to Article 104 of the Federal Constitution, which sets out the multifunctional purpose of agriculture in Switzerland. The popular initiative seeks to place greater emphasis on goal of food security, which is seen as a step backwards for those who supported the AP 2014-17. Further, while the AP 2014-17 represents an important step forward, Swiss agricultural subsidies remain relatively high compared to other OECD countries. The direct payments system still consists of a number of subsidies that have unclear, or possibly contradictory, impacts on environmental objectives. To continue to pursue biodiversity objectives and put Swiss agriculture on a more sustainable footing, the system will need to continue to evolve with better targeted direct payments. The outcome of the pending popular initiative on food security is yet to be seen.

Notes

1. The 4th Global Biodiversity Outlook draws on various sources of information to provide a mid-term assessment of progress towards the implementation of the Strategic Plan for Biodiversity.
2. For example, Article 8.32 of the Agenda 21 programme adopted at the Rio Conference in 1992 states that the signatory countries shall "remove or reduce those subsidies that do not conform with sustainable development objectives", as well as "reform or recast existing structures of economic and fiscal incentives to meet environment and development objectives". The idea of "Restructuring taxation and phasing out harmful subsidies, where they exist" is also found in the Plan of Implementation of the World Summit on Sustainable Development, adopted at Johannesburg in 2002.
3. Aichi Target 3 states: "By 2020, at the latest, incentives, including subsidies, harmful to biodiversity are eliminated, phased out or reformed in order to minimise or avoid negative impacts, and positive incentives for the conservation and sustainable use of biodiversity are developed and applied, consistent and in harmony with the Convention and other relevant international obligations, taking into account national socio economic conditions."
4. WTO "Green Box" criteria include those payments that are allowed without limit. While the process of market-oriented reforms had generally been advancing in a positive direction, Swiss agricultural support remained almost three times the OECD average (WTO, 2013).

References

Butchart et al. (2010), "Global biodiversity: indicators of recent decline", *Science*, 328.

Convention on Biological Diversity (CBD) (2014), *Global Biodiversity Outlook 4, Convention on Biological Diversity*, Montreal, QC.

De Gorter, H. and J. Swinnen (2002), "The political economy of agricultural policy", in *Handbook of Agricultural Economics, Volume 2*, B. Gardner and G. Rausser (eds.), Elsevier Science B.V.

Ekins, P. and R. Salmons (2010), "Making reform happen in environmental policy", in *Making Reform Happen: Lessons from OECD Countries*, OECD Publishing, Paris, *http://dx.doi.org/10.1787/9789264086296-6-en*.

Felder, S. and R. Schleiniger (2002), "Environmental tax reform: efficiency and political feasibility", *Ecological Economics* Vol.42, Elsevier, Amsterdam, pp.107-116.

IMF (2013), *Energy Subsidy Reform: Lessons and Implications*, International Monetary Fund.

OECD (2012), *OECD Environmental Outlook to 2050: The Consequences of Inaction*, OECD Publishing, Paris, *http://dx.doi.org/10.1787/9789264122246-en*.

OECD (2011a), *Towards Green Growth*, OECD Publishing, Paris, *http://dx.doi.org/10.1787/9789264111318-en*.

OECD (2011b), *Fisheries Policy Reform: National Experiences*, OECD Publishing, Paris, *http://dx.doi.org/10.1787/9789264096813-en*.

OECD (2011c), *Evaluation of Agricultural Policy Reforms in the European Union*, OECD Publishing, Paris, *http://dx.doi.org/10.1787/9789264112124-en*.

OECD (2006), *The Political Economy of Environmentally Related Taxes*, OECD Publishing, Paris, *http://dx.doi.org/10.1787/9789264025530-en*.

Potier, D. (2014), "Pesticides et agro-écologie : les champs du possible" [Pesticides and agro-ecology : the range of possibilities], Report from Dominique Potier, deputy of Meurthe et Moselle to the Prime Minister Manuel Valls, November 2014, Paris, *www.dominiquepotier.com/UserFiles/File/rapport-dpotier-pesticides-et-agro-ecologie-basse-def.pdf* (accessed 14 March 2016).

Saint-Ges, V. and M.-C. Belis-Bergouignan (2009), "Ways of reducing pesticides use in Bordeaux vineyards", *Journal of Cleaner Production*, Vol. 17, pp. 1644-1653.

Sainteny, G. (2011), "Public incentives harmful to biodiversity", Report of the commission chaired by Guillaume Sainteny, Centre d'analyse stratégique [Centre of Strategic Analysis].

Sutinen, J.G. (2008), "Major challenges for fishery policy reform: a political economy perspective", *OECD Food, Agriculture and Fisheries Papers*, No. 8, OECD Publishing, Paris, *http://dx.doi.org/10.1787/242275787821*.

Swinnen, J. (2010), "The political economy of agricultural and food policies: recent contributions, new insights, and areas for further research", *Applied Economic Perspectives and Policy*, 32(1), pp. 33-58, *http://dx.doi.org/10.1093/aepp/ppp012*.

The Guardian (2011), "Swiss election sees nationalist party lose share of votes", 23 October 2011, *www.theguardian.com/world/2011/oct/23/swiss-election-nationalist-party-result* (accessed 21 September 2016).

World Bank (2008), *The Political Economy of Policy Reform: Issues and Implications for Policy Dialogue and Development*, Report No. 44288-GLB, World Bank, Washington, DC.

World Trade Organization (WTO) (2013), *Trade Policy Review, Review by the Secretariat: Switzerland and Liechtenstein*, WT/TPR/S/280, 19 March.

Chapter 2

The political economy of environmental and biodiversity relevant policy reform: Key obstacles and examples

This chapter summarises the salient political economy issues that arise in environmental policy reform generally and provides examples of how they may create barriers to biodiversity related policy reforms. It draws on a literature review to identify common obstacles to reform. These include: potential competitiveness impacts, concerns about the distribution of costs and benefits, the influence of vested interests and rent seeking behaviour, as well as the political and social acceptability of reforms.

Introduction

Political economy analysis attempts to examine the political factors that prevent markets, and governments, from achieving efficient outcomes (World Bank, 2008). While there is no single definition of what constitutes "political economy", some of the more salient issues that arise in the political economy of environmental policy are competitiveness, income distribution, vested interests, as well as the political acceptability of reform.[1] These issues are examined in turn below and examples of where these are relevant to biodiversity are reviewed.[2]

2.1. Competitiveness

A commonly cited obstacle to reforming environmental policies is the potentially adverse impacts on competitiveness. This can, in theory, manifest in two ways. First, intensifying environmental stringency will cause firms to incur higher compliance (production) costs, which drives up prices, reduces sales and profit, and can therefore result in at least some decrease in employment and economic health (Morgernstern et al., 2002).

Second, more stringent regulations may cause a competitive disadvantage compared to jurisdictions with lower standards, resulting in a loss of national competitiveness if nationally important sectors or firms are affected (Barker and Kohler, 1996). This creates an incentive for businesses to relocate to these low-standard jurisdictions (i.e., the so-called "pollution haven" effect) (Esty and Geradin, 1998; GFC, 2010), further affecting employment and national competitiveness. The pollution haven dynamic can influence policymaking, creating pressure to ease regulations in an effort to attract investment (the "race to the bottom" effect) or a "regulatory drag" whereby stringency is never increased (Esty and Geradin, 1998).

It is important to note that this does not necessarily mean that the economy as a whole will suffer, but rather that certain sectors may be negatively affected, while others are positively affected[3] (OECD, 2006; Barker and Kohler, 1996).

The literature finds little empirical evidence of environmental regulation causing major economic or job losses (Morgenstern et al., 2002; Barker and Kohler, 1996; Shapiro and Irons, 2011; Albrizio et al., 2014a; Albrizio et al., 2014b) nor mass industry relocations (Konisky, 2007; Woods, 2006; GFC, 2010; Esty, 2011).[4] Rather, relocations have been mostly driven by other factors such as lower labour costs, emerging markets, or lower corporate income taxes (Repetto, 1995;[5] UNESCAP, 2012;[6] Shapiro and Irons, 2011). Other literature suggests there may be small economic losses in the short term, as well as some industry relocation (Lenzen et al., 2012;[7] OECD, 2006;[8] Dechezleprêtre and Sato, 2014).

Woods (2006) suggests that the effects of regulation may be more pronounced for certain industries (e.g. chemical manufacturing) and for small start-up firms, although the specific impacts will depend on the industry's sensitivity to price, the cost of abatement technologies, and the potential for jobs in abatement to replace any lost in the industry itself (Morgernstern, Pizer, and Shih, 2002).

Examples of studies examining competitiveness impacts in sectors or areas more closely related to biodiversity suggest mixed results. ECOTEC (2001) studied the influence of environmental taxes and charges in areas including water abstraction, wastewater, pesticides, fertilisers, and landfills, and found minimal effects on domestic and international competitiveness or on employment. Its case study of a pesticide tax in Sweden found that the tax comprised an average of 8% of the pesticide price, and had likely led to a decrease in pesticide consumption without causing any competitiveness impacts. In Denmark, the same was true even though the pesticide tax comprised a much higher average (37%) of the retail price. While possible adverse impacts on competitiveness have been frequently raised by farmers in the case of the French pesticide tax (see Chapter 3), the current pesticide tax is still very low, comprising about 5% of the pesticide price. In another study on the impact of the introduction of an effluent water tax in the Philippines, while there was some concern regarding potential relocation of firms, this did not appear to manifest in the end (Box 2.1).

Box 2.1. **Effluent water tax in the Philippines**

The Laguna de Bay region spans approximately 3 800 square kilometres and hosts some 13 million inhabitants and 10 000 enterprises (Catelo et al., 2007), including Manila and several smaller cities. As the second-largest lake in Southeast Asia and the largest in the Philippines, it is critically important for fishing and aquaculture, irrigation, power generation, and many other purposes. However, conflicts between water use and allocation, growth and development, and water quality have subjected it to numerous pressures over the last decades, including population expansion, urbanisation, industrialisation, overfishing, deforestation, and garbage dumping. These have caused eutrophication, biodiversity loss, health impacts, and flooding, among other issues (Deltares, n.d.).

In 1997, the Laguna Lake Development Authority instituted an Environmental User Fee System (EUFS) to encourage companies to decrease oxygen pollution as measured by biochemical oxygen demand (BOD). The EUFS consists of a fixed fee to cover administrative costs along with a variable fee based on volume of discharge and BOD load in the discharge. Despite some regulatory inefficiencies, it appears to have caused an 88% decrease in BOD loading from direct discharges of regulated companies (CBD, 2011) between 1997 and 1999 and a continued significant decrease by 2002 (Catelo et al., 2007).

The EUFS was initially applied to only large polluters in specific sectors, but eventually expanded to include smaller establishments and industries as well as farms and some residences. Industry was somewhat resistant and some firms appear to have contemplated relocating, but reconsidered once they were informed the EUFS would eventually extend country-wide (GWP, n.d.). Further expansion is ongoing, and the EUFS is expected to eventually to cover all possible sources of BOD loading as well as other types of pollution (CBD, 2011).

Source: Catelo, M. et al. (2007); CBD (2011); DELTARES (n.d.); GWP (n.d.).

Competitiveness issues may, however, be more relevant in other sectors related to biodiversity. High seas fisheries in particular are considered to be economically unviable without subsidies (GOC, 2013), suggesting that competitiveness losses can be expected by fleets of any nation that decreases subsidies while others do not. Reform can thus be hampered by a lack of international co-ordination, as nations wish to avoid putting their fleets at a disadvantage. Nevertheless, there are examples of successful fisheries reform in the cases of New Zealand (Box 2.2) and Iceland. In the case of Iceland, in addition to the

Box 2.2. **Successful fisheries and agriculture reform in New Zealand**

Fisheries

Subsidy reduction can be packaged with other fundamental policy changes or combined with other changes to the regulatory environment governing an industry to ease the adjustment process. In the case of fisheries in New Zealand, the financial crisis in the mid-1980's created favourable conditions for a major shift in policy towards the sector in the early 1990s. Subsidies were eliminated virtually overnight, a major change in management philosophy was introduced in the form of rights-based management and individual transferable quotas, and there was a minimum buy-out of existing rights. Subsidy reduction alone would not have been sufficient to create a sustainable fishing sector and would have caused substantial financial and social distress. It would also have an impact on fish stocks due to overfishing when fishers increase effort in order to try and cover marginal costs. In New Zealand, fishery subsidy reduction went hand in hand with a shift to a management regime (individual transferable quotas) which helped give those remaining in the fisheries sector a good chance at creating a profitable business environment, while allowing those who wished to leave to be bought out by those who wished to remain. As a result, fish stocks were managed more effectively and in some cases recovered from overexploitation.

Source: OECD (2007).

Agriculture

In the early 1980s, New Zealand began phasing out its agricultural subsidies, as part of an overall strategy to deregulate and otherwise reform public policies affecting key economic sectors (Myers and Kent, 2001). Price support, input subsidies, interest rate concessions, fertiliser subsidies, tax credits, and below-cost services provided by the Ministry of Agriculture were all removed (Johnson, 2001). While there were initial fears of the economic consequences of subsidy removal, farming productivity has actually been growing faster than before subsidy removal (Humphreys et al., 2003).

In the first years of the reforms, rural unemployment rose and farm incomes declined (OECD, 1998). However, land prices reverted to levels comparable to earnings (Johnson, 2001), and incomes eventually recovered: by 1990-92 the real net income for sheep and beef farms had returned to 1984 levels. Export earnings were maintained, though the composition changed (Johnson, 2001) and rural industries shed a significant percentage of jobs (OECD, 1998); nevertheless, the size of the agricultural sector has increased by 40 percent in constant dollar terms since 1986 (Humphreys et al., 2003). Fertiliser use decreased, as did capital expenditure on new plants and equipment; and a reduction in sheep numbers from 70 to 47.4 million led to land reclamation by woodland and shrubbery, improving ecosystem health. Recovery was also aided by diversification into areas such as value-added agricultural production, tourism, small business, technology, horticulture, fruit and vegetable production, and other local industries (OECD, 1998). Total factor productivity growth was approximately 2.5% annually from 1984-2007, compared to 1.5% annually before reforms (Gilmour and Gurung, 2007); agricultural productivity growth increased from 1 percent to 5.9 percent a year (Humphreys et al. 2003), and the effective rate of assistance decreased to -2% of agricultural production compared to a level of 38%, on average, between 1979-1983, indicating that the sector is now taxed (OECD, 1998). In 1984, the total area of private planted forest area was 500,000 hectares, while in 2001 it reached 1.7 million hectares (Humphreys et al., 2003), in part due to land converted from sheep and beef production to sustainable forestry.

Source: Gilmour, B. and R. Gurung (2007); Humphreys, J. et al. (2003); Johnson, R. (2001); Myers, N. and J. Kent (2001); OECD (1998).

introduction of a successful ITQ system, the government more recently also supplemented this with a resource rent tax to help address distributional concerns related to the initial free allocation of quotas (see Chapter 6).

In terms of empirical evidence for the "race to the bottom" phenomenon, Richards (2003) finds evidence for its existence in tropical forestry regulations, where it is catalysed by trade liberalisation, especially in countries with weaker forest governance structures. Woods (2006) also finds some indication of its occurrence in several U.S. states in the context of surface mining regulations, even in the absence of evidence for major investment movement: regulators simply acted on the *potential* that capital may move.

Appropriate compensating policies can help to counter negative effects on sectoral competitiveness. For example, recycling revenues back to business can offset increased compliance charges (Ekins and Speck, 1999; OECD 2006), as can applying border tax adjustments or countervailing duties to level the playing field for imports and exports (Esty and Geradin, 1998; OECD, 2006). Further, even where a sector's output decreases, if compensation is provided by e.g. lowering labour costs such as employers' social security contributions, overall employment levels may not change (Johnstone and Alavalapati, 1998). Sterner and Hoglund (2006) examine revenue recycling using the tax on NOx emissions in Sweden. They find that lower net tax payments as a result of recycling reduces resistance from polluters and make it politically easier to implement a tax rate high enough to provide abatement effects. Revenue recycling has also been used as a way to address concerns from the agricultural sector given the introduction of the French pesticides tax (see Chapter 3).

2.2. Distributional impacts

The expected distribution of costs and benefits of a policy is another important determinant of its political feasibility. Concerns surrounding regressive impacts of environmental policy reform have posed a barrier to progress (Johnstone and Alavalapati, 1998; Kerkhof et al., 2008; Wier et al., 2005; OECD, 2006). Income regressivity occurs when policy changes raise the price of basic goods, which forces low-income households to allocate a higher proportion of their budget to the goods than households higher on the economic scale.

The distributional effects of environmentally related taxes can arise from a variety of channels and have been broadly categorised as (OECD, 2006):

- The *direct distributional* effects on households arising from payment of the tax.
- The *indirect distributional* effects i.e. from price increases on taxed products from firms.
- The effects arising from the use of environmental tax revenues.
- The effects relating to benefits of environmental improvements.

As noted by OECD (2006), most studies on the income distributional impacts of environmental taxes tend to focus on energy and carbon taxation. Analyses of motor fuel and energy taxes (e.g. Bach et al., 2001; EEA, 2011; Fullerton and Heutel, 2007; Kerkhof et al., 2008; Tiezzi, 2005; Wier et al., 2005) find that, in general, the lowest income households bear larger increases in cost incidence.

In terms of policy instruments more directly relevant to biodiversity, the literature indicates mixed results. ECOTEC (2001), for example, found little evidence for concern regarding the distributional impacts of environmental taxes and charges. In contrast, in the Netherlands, two key issues contributing to the cancellation of a groundwater tax in

2011 were that the incidence fell predominantly on a narrow group of tax payers (10 drinking water companies paid nearly 90% of the tax), and that it did not effectively target environmental outcomes (Schuerhoff et al., 2013). In the UK, water charges caused regressivity due to pricing structures unrelated to the quantity of water consumed (EEA, 2011).

According to Von Moltke (2014), in most cases subsidies to fisheries are granted on the basis of valid policy goals and legitimate motives, including promoting development and poverty alleviation. Artisanal fishermen in Ghana, for example, are strongly against fuel subsidy reform because subsidy removal is expected to further increase fishing costs and thereby exacerbate poverty in their communities (Tanner et al., 2014). For payment for ecosystem services (PES) programmes, obstacles that have been encountered with regard to full empowerment of the poor may include high transaction, investment, and education costs; changing food or fuel prices; the opportunity costs of other livelihoods; the exclusion of informal land tenure; or elite capture (OECD, 2013). These are usually caused by inadequate attention to safeguards for empowering smallholders, agroforestry tenants, and ensuring an equitable distribution of benefits.

Concerns about distributional implications have also been raised in the context of individually transferrable quotas (ITQs). Such concerns in the U.S. for example, led to a moratorium on moving additional fisheries into ITQ programmes that lasted from 1996 to 2004 (Chu, 2008).[9] However, a study by Brandt (2005) examining the equity implications of a regulatory change from command-and-control approaches to ITQs for the mid-Atlantic clam found that no segment of the industry was disproportionately adversely affected by the change. Similarly, in New Zealand, a study notes: "While it is clear that the number of small fishers has fallen since the introduction of the QMS (New Zealand's ITQ-based "Quota Management System") it appears that they, as a group, have been successful in finding alternative employment. From an employment perspective there is no evidence that New Zealand fishers have experienced significant social costs of restructuring the fishery." (Stewart et al., 2006).

Finally, it is also important to ensure that any removal of subsidies does not lead to unintended outcomes that may be worse. For example, small-scale farmers are often dependent on agricultural subsidies, and may thus be forced to expand slash-and-burn agriculture when subsidies are removed, thereby causing more deforestation (Shandra et al., 2011).

In cases where the distributional impacts are likely to be a concern, appropriate policy packages can help to ease the transition. Recycling the revenue raised e.g. from taxes or subsidy removal through income or labour tax reductions can reduce, and may almost completely eliminate, the distributional effects, depending on the chosen method of implementation (Johnstone and Alavalapati, 1998). For example, the regressive impacts of water charges in Spain are offset by the progressive impacts of motor fuel taxes (EEA, 2011).

In Indonesia, the successful removal of pesticides subsidies, despite strong political opposition, has been attributed to taking advantage of fiscal or other policy crises ("policy windows") to improve reform outcomes, and to supporting programmes and political economy conditions (e.g. decentralisation or support for budget reductions) that aided in implementation and in gaining popular support (CBD, 2011) (Box 2.3).

Box 2.3. **The removal of pesticide subsidies in Indonesia**

During the 1970s and 1980s, Indonesia's agricultural policy promoted the use of high-yield crops and associated pesticides through direct subsidies on sales, credit concessions, and government spraying. Excessive usage of these pesticides in rice production caused biodiversity, health, and crop degradation, culminating in USD 1.5 billion worth of rice crop losses in the mid-1980s (CBD, 2011). These were a direct result of brown planthopper infestations, caused by pesticides eradicating the natural insect diversity that kept it in check.

In response, the government removed pesticide subsidies in 1986, and followed by ending fertiliser subsidies in 1996. Although there was strong initial resistance from some farmers, the government simultaneously introduced an integrated pest management system to train farmers in alternative pest control methods, and decentralised agricultural research to the provincial level (CBD, 2011). This helped to create a conducive policy environment for enacting the subsidy reforms, although it should be noted that budget stresses caused by oil price decreases also helped justify cuts (CBD, 2011). The policy package has been very successful: evidence indicates that the combination of technology dissemination and subsidy elimination reduced pesticide demand by 50 percent, saving the government some USD 100 million, while rice production still grew by three million tonnes over the next four years (de Moor and Calamai, 1997), though some of the growth can be attributed to increased fertiliser use (Gallagher, 2001).

Source: CBD (2011); De Moor, A. and P. Calamai (1997); Gallagher (2001).

2.3. Vested interests and rent seeking behaviour

The influence of vested interests and rent seeking behaviour has also been cited as hindrances to environmental fiscal reform (Robin et al., 2003). Politically, reform "often involves trading off the concentrated benefits of vested interests against greater, but more widely dispersed, benefits to the public at large" (OECD, 2007) – in other words, calls for reform are likely to be far more dispersed than pressure to maintain the status quo. It has been noted for example that efforts to place a cap on biofuels in EU renewable energy targets, due to concerns of biofuel production causing increased deforestation, have been subject to heavy lobbying by the biofuels industry, causing legislative delays (EurActiv, 2013). In the case of fisheries, the overall lack of subsidy reform has also been attributed, at least in part, to interest group politics, since the fishing industry often enjoys a high level of influence domestically and in regional fishery management organisations (RFMOs) (GOC, 2013).

A number of other cases that have direct or indirect implications for biodiversity have been documented. For example, Swinnen (2010) finds that multiple EU Common Agricultural Policy (CAP) reform efforts have been impeded by farm interests, and American farming associations have been found to "significantly influence" agricultural subsidies through lobbying (Alvarez, 2005). American sugar producers have been so effective at mobilising lobbying networks that they have "[generated] unmatched levels of legislative support", which has enabled them to enjoy increased protection even as other agricultural support mechanisms are dismantled (Alvarez, 2005). In Florida, this has resulted in the diversion of water from the Everglades; when returned to the watershed, it is loaded with fertiliser run-off that causes eutrophication (Robin et al., 2003). In Belgium, lobbying-driven exemptions for farmers from a pesticide tax led to the failure of the tax (ECOTEC, 2001). Also, in India, states in which wealthy farming groups hold major influence over the political agenda find it difficult to increase electricity prices to prevent groundwater overuse (World Bank, 2005).

Furthermore, "many reforms are designed to reduce or eliminate the rents accruing to small groups of privileged interests ... however, these are precisely the policies that are most likely to be fought" (World Bank, 2008). The inflated rents reaped by these entities as a result of their efforts derive not only from capture of subsidies or grants, but also from lowered taxes, less stringent investment regulations (OECD, 2007), and foregone valuations of ecosystem services and biodiversity. The case study of Iceland (Chapter 6) is an example of a recent policy reform (via the additional introduction of a resource rent tax) specifically designed to allocate a greater share of the resource rents from the harvesting of a common property resource to the general public.

The resources at the disposal of rent seeking parties also allow them to be well focused, especially as compared to opponents who do not have the time or money to organise as efficiently (OECD, 2007). They may manipulate the legislative process to obtain advantageous results, which helps them create increased revenue and pressure the political process even more: "[subsidies] themselves create a pool of money out of which recipients can influence the very political process that channels money to them in the first place" (Steenblik, 1998). In Laos for example, illegal rent seeking is pervasive due to the structure of the permitting process and estimates suggest that bribes for permit approvals comprise logging companies' single largest expense (Baird, 2009).

2.4. Political acceptability of reform

Increasing the stringency of environmental regulations or eliminating harmful subsidies is a process subject to complex political considerations that increase the difficulty of obtaining support. Societal conditions may influence the behaviour of elected officials, who feel the need to provide positive economic news; maintaining the status quo thus becomes politically attractive (OECD, 2005) and they may relax regulations or block more stringent policies to encourage business (Konisky, 2007). Other acceptability problems include distrust of government (OECD, 2006; Withana et al., 2012) and conceptual barriers: the public may not trust that the proposed tool will be as effective as claimed, or that the government will not appropriate revenue for other uses. In some cases, even though awareness may be high, the public may have trouble understanding the solution – e.g. a shift of taxes from income to pollutants (OECD, 2006).

Political acceptance is also dependent on (among other concerns) the perceived effectiveness of the policy, the degree of fairness, and the degree of awareness of the problem being addressed (OECD, 2006). For example, Soderholm and Christiernsson (2008) examine the political acceptance of fertiliser taxes in Austria, Denmark, the Netherlands, Norway, and Sweden. They find that the choice of tax scheme design matters not only for the cost effectiveness of the policy, but can also be an important mean of reducing any political opposition towards environmental taxes. They state: *The European experience in fertiliser taxation indicates that some kind of earmarking of tax revenues can be effective in increasing the legitimacy of the tax policy, and taxes which achieve a close proportionality to damage done will often be perceived as fair.*

Fairness most often concerns distributional or competitiveness impacts, but often the public may not be aware of any compensating mechanisms, or does not understand that policies are typically intended to assign responsibility to those who have contributed to the problem. Awareness is also subject to several secondary factors, including visibility of the issue (plastic bag pollution vs. biodiversity loss, for example); the ability to create a convincing narrative; and the ability to deploy messaging effectively. Narratives in fact play a major role: environmentally harmful industries have been particularly adept at creating "false perceptions and fear of change" about potential societal damage (Withana et al., 2012), framing reforms as competitiveness-reducing initiatives and thereby decreasing acceptability. Similarly, subsidy recipients often exaggerate the benefits to society of the support they receive (OECD, 2007). In some cases, social mores may influence the level of support granted, as for agriculture, which is often seen as an "old" and "traditional" industry that has provided much employment (van Beers and van den Bergh, 2001) and is therefore deserving of ongoing protection. This is also the case in Switzerland.

Regional laws can also hamper domestic ability for reform, as is occasionally the case in the EU. For example, the Euroviginette Directive does not allow Member States to account for impacts on biodiversity, landscapes, forestry, water, or other natural resources in determining road charges; the requirement for unanimity in the Council on tax-related measures may restrict reform progress; and feed-in tariffs for firewood-based cogenerated electricity in Estonia, implemented in support of EU directives, may cause overharvesting (DEFRA, 2012; Withana et al., 2012).

Notes

1. The literature on political economy of environmental reform covers several elements and sometimes uses different terms to describe similar issues. OECD (2006) for example examines competitiveness, income distribution, administrative costs, and political acceptance as the major political economy factors surrounding environmental taxes. De Gorter and Swinnen (2002) consider the influences of individual and politicians' preferences, collective lobbying, and institutions, whereas special interest effects, voter ignorance, issue bundling, politician short-sightedness, de-coupling of costs and benefits, and bureaucratic inefficiencies are examined by Sutinen (2008). Other issues raised include administrative agency and discipline (World Bank, 2008; Haggard and Webb, 1993); crisis points (or lack thereof) (Haggard and Webb, 1993); external influences (Haggard and Webb, 1993); government trustworthiness or transparency (World Bank, 2008; DFID, 2004); income inequality (Høj et al., 2006); information deficiencies (IMF, 2013); institutional structures and rules (Acosta and Petit, 2013); property rights (Leal, 2010); reform timing (Haggard and Webb, 1993); strength and type of government (Haggard and Webb, 1993); trade (Leal, 2010); and vested interests and rent-seeking behaviour (World Bank, 2008; IMF, 2013; Haggard and Webb, 1993). Income distribution and income inequality are similar issues, as are crisis points and reform timing. This chapter addresses the most prominent issues addressed in the political economy of environmental reform.
2. It is important to note that comprehensive and comparable information on recent biodiversity-relevant policy reforms do not readily exist. Various studies have been undertaken to review progress in this domain such as the 2008 OECD Report on the Implementation of the 2004 Council Recommendation on the Use of Economic Instruments in Promoting the Conservation and Sustainable Use of Biodiversity. This found that although progress had been made with regard to subsidies that aim to promote biodiversity, much less progress had been made with regard to the introduction of instruments such as taxes, fees, and charges (i.e. those instruments that aim to internalise the negative external costs of production and consumption) or the reform of environmentally harmful subsidies (OECD, 2008a). A recent biodiversity tagging exercise of the OECD database on Policy Instruments on the Environment (PINE), finds that there are currently more than 400 instruments in place that are biodiversity relevant in the OECD and 35 non-OECD countries that provide information to this database.
3. For example, increased employment may be created in pollution-abating industries or in firms which are more easily able to comply with the regulations (Shapiro and Irons, 2011; Morgenstern, Pizer, and Shih, 2002; Dechezleprêtre and Sato, 2014).
4. These studies tend to focus on pulp and paper mills, plastic manufacturers, iron and steel mills, food and food products, chemicals, cement, and other manufacturing industries.
5. For the manufacturing sector, particularly pulp and paper, petroleum; organic and inorganic chemicals; coal mining; fertilisers; cement production; ferrous and non-ferrous metal production; metal manufacturers; and wood producers. Relocations due to labour cost differences occurred in

industries such as textiles, apparel, footwear, and other light manufacturers, or producers of consumption items such as Coke.

6. For EU carbon and energy taxes.
7. For commodities directly impacting biodiversity, such as coffee growing or forestry. Also see Meyfroidt, P. et al. (2013), "Globalization of land use: distant drivers of land change and geographic displacement of land use", Current Opinion in Environmental Sustainability, Vol. 5/5, pp. 438-444.
8. For steel or other carbon-intensive production.
9. A report from the National Research Council was requested, and subsequently delivered in 1999, which recommended that Congress should lift the moratorium (NRC, 1999).

References

Acosta, A.M. and Jethro Petit (2013), "Practice Guide: A Combined Approach to Political Economy and Power Analysis", *Work in Progress Paper*, Institute of Development Studies.

Albrizio, S. et al. (2014a), "Do environmental policies matter for productivity growth?: Insights from new cross-country measures of environmental policies", *OECD Economics Department Working Papers*, No. 1176, OECD Publishing, Paris, *http://dx.doi.org/10.1787/5jxrjncjrcxp-en*.

Albrizio, S. et al. (2014b), "Empirical evidence on the effects of environmental policy stringency on productivity growth", *OECD Economics Department Working Papers*, No. 1179, OECD Publishing, Paris, *http://dx.doi.org/10.1787/5jxrjnb36b40-en*.

Alvarez, J. (2005), "Sweetening the US legislature: the remarkable success of the sugar lobby", *The Political Quarterly*, Vol.76/1, pp. 92-99.

Bach, S. et al. (n.d.), *The Effects of the Ecological Tax Reform in Germany*, DIW Berlin, *www.czp.cuni.cz/ekoreforma/EDR/Mayer%20DIW%20abstr.pdf* (accessed 28 November 2014).

Baird, I. (2009), *Quotas, Powers, Patronage, and Illegal Rent-Seeking: The Political Economy of Logging and the Timber Trade In Southern Laos*, Forest Trends.

Barker, T. and J. Köhler (1996), "Environmental policy and competitiveness", *Environmental Policy Research Briefs*, Number 6, The European Union Research Network on Market-Based Instruments for Sustainable Development.

Brandt, S. (2005), "The equity debate: distributional impacts of individual transferable quotas", *Ocean & Coastal Management*, Vol. 48, pp. 15-30.

Catelo, M. et al. (2007), *Impact Evaluation of the Environmental User Fee System: A Stakeholder Perspective*, Economy and Environment Program for South East Asia.

CBD (2014), *Global Biodiversity Outlook 4*, Convention on Biological Diversity, Montreal, QC.

CBD (2011), "Incentive measures for the conservation and sustainable use of biological diversity", *CBD Technical Series*, No. 56, Convention on Biological Diversity, Montreal, QC.

Chu, C. (2008), "Thirty years later: The global growth of ITQs and their influence on stock status in marine fisheries", *Fish and Fisheries*, Vol. 10/2, pp. 217-230.

Colchester, M. et al. (2006), *Promised Land: Palm Oil and Land Acquisition in Indonesia – Implications for Local Communities and Indigenous Peoples*, Forest Peoples Programme, Moreton-in-Marsh, England.

De Moor, A. and P. Calamai (1997), *Subsidizing Unsustainable Development: Undermining the Earth with Public Funds*, Earth Council.

De Gorter, H. and J. Swinnen (2002), "The political economy of agricultural policy", in *Handbook of Agricultural Economics, Volume 2*, B. Gardner and G. Rausser (eds.), Elsevier Science B.V.

Dechezleprêtre, A. and M. Sato (2014), *The Impacts of Environmental Regulations on Competitiveness*, Policy Brief, Grantham Research Institute on Climate Change and the Environment, London School of Economics, London, UK.

DELTARES (n.d.), *Sustainable Development of the Laguna de Bay Environment*.

DFID (2004), "The political economy of fishery fiscal reforms", *Fiscal Reform in Fisheries*, Key Sheet #6, Department for International Development, London, UK.

EEA (2011), "Environmental tax reform in Europe: implications for income distribution", *EEA Technical Report*, No.16/2011, European Environmental Agency, Copenhagen.

Ekins, P. and S. Speck (1999), "Competitiveness and exemptions from environmental taxes in Europe", *Environmental and Resource Economics*, Vol. 13, pp.369-396.

Esty, D. (2011), "Economic integration and environmental protection", in *The Global Environment*, 3rd Edition, R. Axelrod et al. (eds), CQ Press.

Esty, D. and D. Gerardin (1998), "Environmental protection and international competitiveness: A conceptual framework", *Faculty Scholarship Series,* Paper 445, Yale Law School, New Haven, CT.

DEFRA (2012), *Incentive Measures and Biodiversity – Rapid Review and Guidance Development*, Department for Environment, Food, and Rural Affairs, London, UK.

ECOTEC (2001), *Study on the Economic and Environmental Implications of the Use of Environmental Taxes and Charges in the European Union and its Member States*, Birmingham, UK.

EurActiv (2013), "Biofuels industry sent 'three mails an hour' in ILUC lobby offensive", EurActiv.com, *www.euractiv.com/energy/biofuels-industry-sent-mails-hou-news-519531*, accessed December 23, 2014.

Felder, S. and R. Schleiniger (2002), "Environmental tax reform: Efficiency and political feasibility", *Ecological Economics* Vol.42, Elsevier, Amsterdam, pp.107-116.

Fullerton, D., and G. Heutel (2007), "The general equilibrium incidence of environmental taxes", *Journal of Public Economics*, Vol. 91, pp. 571-591.

Gallagher (2001), *Stopping Subsidies for Pesticides in Indonesian Rice Production*, Sustainable Development International.

Gilmour, B. and R. Gurung (2007), "New Zealand agriculture policy review", *Policy Note*, Agriculture and Agri-Food Canada.

GFC (2010), "Competitiveness and environmental tax reform", *GFC Briefing Paper*, No. 7, Green Fiscal Commission, London, UK.

GOC (2013), "Elimination of harmful fisheries subsidies affecting the high seas", *Policy Options Paper #6*, Global Ocean Commission.

Grainger, C. and D. Parker (2013), "The political economy of fishery reform", *Annual Review of Resource Economics*, Vol. 5, pp.369-386.

GWP (n.d.), "Philippines: establishing an industrial wastewater effluent fee program, Laguna de Bay", Case Study, No. 82, Global Water Partnership.)

Haggard, S. and S. Webb (1993), "What do we know about the political economy of economic policy reform?", *The World Bank Research Observer*, Vol. 8/2, Washington, DC, pp.143-168.

Høj, J. et al. (2006), "The political economy of structural reform: empirical evidence from OECD countries", *OECD Economics Department Working Papers*, No. 501, OECD Publishing, Paris, *http://dx.doi.org/10.1787/881353527404*.

Humphreys, J.et al. (2003), "Greening farm subsidies", *RIRDC Publication* No. 03/040, Rural Industries Research and Development Corporation, Canberra.

IMF (2013), *Energy Subsidy Reform: Lessons and Implications*, International Monetary Fund.

Indrarto, G. et al. (2012), "The context of REDD+ in Indonesia: drivers, agents, and institutions", *Working Paper* 92, CIFOR, Bogor, Indonesia.

Johnson, R. (2001), *New Zealand's Agriculture Reforms and their International Implications*, Institute of Economic Affairs, London.

Johnstone, N. and J. Alavalapati (1998), "The distributional effects of environmental tax reform", *Discussion Paper*, No. 98-01, International Institute for Environment and Development, London, UK.

Kerkhof, A. et al. (2008), "Taxation of multiple greenhouse gases and the effects on income distribution", *Ecological Economics*, Vol. 67, pp. 318-326.

Konisky, D. (2007), "Regulatory competition and environmental enforcement: Is there a race to the bottom?", *American Journal of Political Science*, Vol. 51/4, pp. 853-872.

Kostka, G. (2014), "Barriers to the implementation of environmental policies at the local level in China", *Policy Research Working Papers*, No. 7016, World Bank Development Research Group.

Leal, D. (ed.) (2010), *The Political Economy of Natural Resource Use: Lessons for Fisheries Reform*, The World Bank, Washington, DC.

Lenzen, M. et al. (2012), "International trade drives biodiversity threats in developing nations", *Nature*, Vol. 486/7401, pp. 109-112.

Morgenstern, R. et al. (2002), "Jobs versus the environment: An industry-level perspective", *Journal of Environmental Economics and Management*, Vol.43, pp. 412-436.

Myers, N. and J. Kent (2001), *Perverse Subsidies: How Tax Dollars Can Undercut the Environment and the Economy*, Island Press, Washington, DC.

NRC (1999), *Sharing the Fish: Toward a National Policy on Individual Fishing Quotas*, Committee to review individual fishing quotas, National Academy Press, Washington, DC.

OECD (2013), *Scaling-up Finance Mechanisms for Biodiversity*, OECD Publishing, Paris, *http://dx.doi.org/10.1787/9789264193833-en*.

OECD (2008), *Report on Implementation of the 2004 Council Recommendation on the Use of Economic Instruments in Promoting the Conservation and Sustainable Use of Biodiversity* [ENV/EPOC/GSP/BIO(2008)1/FINAL], OECD Publishing, Paris.

OECD (2007), *Subsidy Reform and Sustainable Development: Political Economy Aspects*, OECD Publishing, Paris, *http://dx.doi.org/10.1787/9789264019379-en*.

OECD (2006), *The Political Economy of Environmentally Related Taxes*, OECD Publishing, Paris, *http://dx.doi.org/10.1787/9789264025530-en*.

OECD (2005), *Environmentally Harmful Subsidies: Challenges for Reform*, OECD Publishing, Paris, *http://dx.doi.org/10.1787/9789264012059-en*.

OECD (1998), *Agricultural Policy Reform and the Rural Economy in OECD Countries*, OECD Publishing, Paris, *http://dx.doi.org/10.1787/9789264162532-en*.

Repetto, R. (1995), *Jobs, Competitiveness, and Environmental Regulation: What are the Real Issues?*, World Resources Institute, Washington, DC.

Richards, M. et al. (2003), "Higher international standards or rent-seeking race to the bottom? The impacts of forest product trade liberalisation on forest governance", *Impact Assessment of Forest Products Trade in Promotion of Sustainable Forest Management*, Background paper, GCP/INT/775/JPN, FAO, Rome.

Robin, S. et al. (2003), "Perverse Subsidies and the implications for biodiversity: a review of recent findings and the status of policy reforms", *Sustainable Finance Stream*, 5th World Parks Congress, Durban, South Africa.

Schuerhoff, M. et al. (2013), "The life and death of the Dutch groundwater tax", *Water Policy*, Vol. 15, pp. 1064-1077.

Shandra, J. et al. (2011), "World Bank lending and deforestation: a cross-national analysis", *International Sociology*, Vol. 26/3, pp. 292-314.

Shapiro, I. and J. Irons (2011), "Regulation, employment, and the economy", *EPI Briefing Paper*, No. 305, Economic Policy Institute, Washington, DC.

Swinnen, J. (2010), "The political economy of the most radical reform of the Common Agricultural Policy", Supplement: Perspectives on International Agricultural Policy, *German Journal of Agricultural Economics*, Vol. 59.

Steenblik, R. (1998), "Previous multilateral efforts to discipline subsidies to natural resource based industries", *Report of Proceedings on Workshop on the Impact of Government Financial Transfers on Fisheries Management, Resource Sustainability, and International Trade*, Vol. 17.

Sterner, T. and L. Isaksson (2006), "Refunded emission payments theory, distribution of costs, and Swedish experience of NO_x abatement", *Ecological Economics*, Vol. 57, pp. 93-106.

Soderholm, P. and A. Christiernsson (2008), "Policy effectiveness and acceptance in the taxation of environmentally damaging chemical compounds", *Environmental Science and Policy*, Vol. 11, pp. 240-252.

Sutinen, J.G. (2008), "Major challenges for fishery policy reform: a political economy perspective", *OECD Food, Agriculture and Fisheries Papers*, No. 8, OECD Publishing, Paris, *http://dx.doi.org/10.1787/242275787821*.

Tanner, T. et al. (2014), "Political economy of climate compatible development: artisanal fisheries and climate change in Ghana", *IDS Working Paper*, No. 446, Institute of Development Studies, London, UK.

Tiezzi, S. (2005), "The welfare effects and the distributive impact of carbon taxation on Italian households", *Energy Policy*, Vol. 33, pp. 1567-1612.

UNESCAP (2012), "Fact sheet – environmental tax reform and competitiveness", *Low Carbon Green Growth Roadmap for Asia and the Pacific.*

Van Beers, C. and J. van den Bergh (2001), "Perseverance of perverse subsidies and their impact on trade and environment", *Ecological Economics*, Vol.36, pp. 475-486.

Von Moltke, A. (ed.) (2014). *Fisheries Subsidies, Sustainable Development, and the World Trade Organisation*, Routledge.

Wier, M. et al. (2005), "Are CO_2 taxes regressive? Evidence from the Danish experience", *Ecological Economics*, Vol. 52, pp. 239-251.

Withana, S. et al. (2012), *Study Supporting the Phasing Out of Environmentally Harmful Subsidies*, Institute for European Environmental Policy (IEEP), Institute for Environmental Studies – Vrije Universiteit (IVM), Ecologic Institute and Vision on Technology (VITO) for the European Commission – DG Environment, Brussels, Belgium.

Woods, N. (2006), "Interstate competition and environmental regulation: A test of the race-to-the-bottom thesis", *Social Science Quarterly*, Vol. 87/1, pp. 174-189.

World Bank (2008), *The Political Economy of Policy Reform: Issues and Implications for Policy Dialogue and Development*, Report No. 44288-GLB, World Bank, Washington, DC.

World Bank (2005), *Environmental Fiscal Reform: WhatSshould be Done and How to Achieve it*, World Bank, Washington, DC.

Chapter 3

The evolution of the tax on pesticides and the pesticide savings certificates in France

This chapter examines the evolution of the tax on pesticides and the recent introduction of the pesticide savings certificates in France. The analysis takes a political economy perspective to identify potential barriers to reform that were encountered and if and how they were overcome. This case study illustrates how potential competitiveness impacts may or may not influence reform, the benefits of broad stakeholder engagement and how a solid evidence base can help the government resist the influence of vested interests.

Introduction

As the leading agricultural producer in the European Union (EU), France is a major user of pesticides. The use of pesticides supports agricultural production but also contributes to environmental degradation and risks to human health. The first tax on pesticides was introduced in France in 1999, later replaced by a tax on diffuse pollution in 2008, which applies to pesticide sales. The tax rate has increased moderately over the years and the tax base has expanded to cover a greater number of harmful substances. However, competitiveness concerns limited more significant increases in the tax rate. The resulting low level of the tax has not provided a sufficiently strong incentive to reduce use, and the ambitious goal to reduce pesticide use by half has not been reached. Indeed, pesticide use has continued to rise. The recent adoption of a novel instrument, pesticide savings certificates, represents a compromise with the agricultural sector, which opposed stricter regulation or a further increase in the tax rate on pesticides.

This case study examines the political economy dimension of these reforms. It highlights the importance of addressing potential competitiveness impacts, the benefits of broad stakeholder engagement and how a solid evidence base to support the reform can help the government to stand firm against lobbying pressure.

3.1. Impact of agricultural pesticide use on biodiversity in France

Like other countries in Western Europe, in France, agriculture is a major anthropogenic pressure on biodiversity (OECD, 2016). Pesticides[1] (also referred to as plant protection products) are considered one of the main drivers of the decline in biodiversity in industrialised countries. France is the second largest user of pesticides in Europe in terms of total volume[2] (after Spain) (Marcus and Simon, 2015) and was the eighth largest consumer worldwide in 2010 (OECD, 2016). This level of consumption needs to be considered in the context of the level of agricultural production in France (18% of production in the EU) and the agricultural surface used (16% of the agricultural surface in the EU) (Marcus and Simon, 2015). Overall, the situation has not improved much since 2000 (OECD, 2016). The most recent data on national pesticide use from the French Ministry of Agriculture, Food and Forest (MAAF) report a 5.8% increase between the period 2011-13 and the period 2012-14, with a striking increase of 9.4% between 2013 and 2014 (MAAF, 2016a).[3]

The use of pesticides supports agricultural production by reducing potential harm to crops caused by pests and disease, thus enabling a more consistent yield. However, it also contributes to environmental degradation, with the presence of pesticides in surface and groundwater, soil and in the air resulting in negative consequences for terrestrial and aquatic biodiversity as well as human health.[4] Pesticides in the environment can present a particular threat for biodiversity, especially due to their negative impact on species important for the food chain, including pollinators, which are critical for the production of fruits and vegetables (Marcus and Simon, 2015). Pesticides have been shown to cause losses in species richness, even in concentrations that current European legislation considers "environmentally protective" (Beketov et al., 2013). A study of the intensification of agricultural production in Europe concluded that, despite decades of policy aiming to ban harmful pesticides, the negative effects of pesticides on wild plant and animal species persist and also reduce opportunities for biological pest control (Geiger et al., 2010). With regard to human health impacts, pesticides have been associated with several diseases, notably cancer, neurological diseases and difficulties with reproduction (Marcus and Simon, 2015; Green Economy Committee, 2015).

In 2013, pesticides were present at 92% of measuring points for rivers and streams and 69% of measuring points for groundwater bodies in France (SOeS, 2016). While the presence of pesticides in groundwater is generally less prevalent than in surface water, they can accumulate over time, remaining in groundwater for decades. In 2013, the total concentration of pesticides exceeded quality standards in 21.6% of the measuring points for groundwater and 5.1% for rivers and streams (SOeS, 2016).

There are a number of studies that aim to quantify the benefits of pesticides by estimating the productivity of pesticide use, with highly variable results[5] (Bourguet and Guillemaud, 2016). However, most of these studies do not consider the related negative externalities of pesticide use. In France, the total costs of the negative consequences of pesticide use on the environment and human health have yet to be fully evaluated (Green Economy Committee, 2015). Recent studies on the economic costs of pesticide use in the United States and the EU indicate that these costs are substantial. The French National Institute for Agricultural Research (INRA) highlights that these costs could be very significant, estimating the "hidden" and external costs[6] of pesticide use in the United States at USD 39.5 billion per year at the end of the 1980s and early 1990s (Bourguet and Guillemaud, 2016). In the EU, the annual health and economic costs related to endocrine-disrupting chemicals is estimated at EUR 157 billion, with pesticides accounting for the largest share of these costs at around EUR 120 billion (Trasande et al., 2015).

A study examining the cost to households in France of the impacts of diffuse pollution from agriculture (from pesticides and nitrogen fertiliser) on drinking water estimated the cost at between EUR 1 billion and EUR 1.5 billion annually (Bommelaer and Devaux, 2011). Of this, the costs borne by local authorities for water purification required to treat pesticides is estimated at between EUR 260 and 360 million annually, with the additional cost of purifying drinking water to treat the presence of 1 kilogramme of pesticides estimated at EUR 60 000 (Bommelaer and Devaux, 2011).

Increasing pressure on policymakers to address pesticide pollution

In France, policymakers have come under increasing pressure to address pesticide pollution (Saint-Ges and Belis-Bergouignan, 2009). According to a recent perception survey, risks related to pesticides are the second most worrying environmental risk for the French population (after air pollution) (ISRN, 2015). Heightened attention in the media, studies linking pesticide exposure to disease, as well as a recent court ruling linking a farmer's sickness to pesticide exposure (Cour d'Appel of Lyon, 2015) continues to alert farmers and the public, especially those living near agricultural sites, to potential risks.

At the same time, France is Europe's leading agricultural producer[7] with powerful agricultural unions (including the *Fédération Nationale des Syndicats d'Exploitants d'Agricoles* (FNSEA); the *Confédération Paysanne*; *Jeunes Agriculteurs*) and a dominance of rural representation in the Senate (the upper house of Parliament in France). The *Chambres d'agriculture*[8] work closely with farmers, providing technical advice about the growing process. They tend to be conservative in their approach, but have the potential to be influential in the diffusion of more ecologically-friendly practices.

While knowledge of the potentially negative impacts of pesticides has been in the public sphere for over a decade, the extent to which public pressure has been sufficiently strong to influence policy decisions at the national level and provide a counterweight to other political pressures, including the agricultural lobby, is a matter of debate. Over the course of the past decade, the influence of public pressure on policy is difficult to trace, but more recently, increased media attention, campaigns by NGOs and swelling public pressure has appeared to give momentum to further action on specific types of pesticides. A notable example is the French Parliament's ratification in June 2016 of a ban on neonicotinoids (insecticides with harmful impacts on bee populations) starting in 2018. Strong public pressure and concerted engagement from the Minister of Ecology helped to push for policy action on this issue.

Overall, there are multiple forces driving policy reform on pesticide use in France. Some argue that the main driver of reform in this area has been the necessity to meet objectives under the relevant EU Directives and Regulations on pesticides and environmental quality, in particular the Directive on the Sustainable Use of Pesticides (Directive 2009/128/EC), the Regulation on Plant Protection Product Authorisations (EC Regulation No. 1107/2009) and the EU Water Framework Directive (Directive 2000/60/EC). Others point to the elevated attention in the media and action by NGOs, which have contributed to a more aware and knowledgeable general public. An important driver is undoubtedly the French population demonstrating its preferences through market choices, e.g. the growing demand for organic products and their willingness to pay a premium for them.

3.2. The evolution of the tax on pesticides

The general tax on polluting activities

The first tax applied to pesticides in France was introduced in 1999 under the framework of the general tax on polluting activities (*taxe générale sur les activités polluantes*) (TGAP). The tax was applied to substances contained in commercial products classified as dangerous, including pesticides. The tax had two stated objectives: to provide an incentive to industry to develop less toxic alternatives and to provide an incentive for farmers to purchase and use less toxic products (ORP, 2015). In addition, it also served to raise revenue. The tax rate varied according to the toxicity of the pesticide, with seven categories of products identified and tax rates ranging from EUR 381 per tonne to 1 677 per tonne. With the adoption of this tax, France became one of the few OECD countries (along with Denmark, Norway, Sweden and the United States) with taxes on either fertilisers or pesticides.

Setting an ambitious pesticide use reduction target

In 2007, an ambitious target to reduce pesticide use by half ("if possible") by 2018 was among the outcomes of the comprehensive, multi-stakeholder process *Grenelle de l'environnement* (the Grenelle Forum).[9] The Grenelle Forum set an important precedent for stakeholder engagement in environmental issues in France. It founded a new model of environmental governance built among five stakeholder groups, involving the government, elected local representatives, business employers, unions and NGOs. Through its broad participatory approach, this five-part governance system[10] lends greater credibility to the commitments made on environmental issues (OECD, 2016). Although a time and resource intensive process, Grenelle is credited with helping to set more ambitious objectives for pesticide reduction (along with other environmental goals) than might have otherwise been the case.[11]

Drawing on the "Grenelle model" of governance, a broad participatory approach was used in the development of the Ecophyto Plan, which was initiated in 2008 to support the pesticide use reduction target. The Plan developed a set of actions to manage risks from pesticide use, monitor impacts, and reduce cropping systems' dependence on pesticides (OECD, 2012). These actions include better monitoring of use and risks, research and development for alternatives to pesticide use, and information and communication campaigns.

The tax on diffuse agricultural pollution

In 2008, the TGAP on pesticides was replaced by a tax on diffuse agricultural pollution with the entry into force of the Law on water and the freshwater environment (*loi sur l'eau et les milieux aquatiques*) (LEMA). The law introduced seven "water taxes" (including the tax on diffuse pollution), which are collected by the six Water Agencies (*les agences de l'eau*).

The tax on diffuse pollution is levied on the sale of pesticides, with the rate varying according to toxicity of the substance (Table 3.1).[12] Tax rates for pesticide in other OECD countries are summarised in Annex 3.A1. In France, the tax is paid by farmers and collected by distributors of pesticides (rather than by manufacturers and importers) in order to make it more visible to farmers (Bommelear and Devaux, 2012). The ceiling on the diffuse pollution tax rate is determined by legislators, established in the environmental law (Cour des comptes, 2015).

Table 3.1. **Evolution of the ceiling on the diffuse pollution tax rate (2008-11) (in EUR/tonne)**

Category of substance	2008	2009	2010	Since 2011
Substances which are very toxic, toxic, carcinogenic, mutagenic or toxic to reproduction	2.25	3.7	4.4	5.1
Substances which are hazardous for the environment	0.9	1.5	1.7	2
Mineral chemicals which are hazardous for the environment	0.38	0.6	0.7	0.9

Source: Marcus and Simon, 2015.

The rate of the diffuse pollution tax was raised several times between 2008 and 2011. At present, however, the tax rate for the most toxic substances still only amounts to around 5% or 6% of the sale price of pesticides, which strongly limits its effectiveness as an incentive to reduce use (OECD, 2016). The increase in the tax rate was mainly driven by the need to raise revenue to finance the Ecophyto plan (Potier, 2014). The total revenue from the tax increased from EUR 100 million in 2011 to EUR 110 million in 2014 (Marcus and Simon, 2015). The amount of tax revenue channelled to the Ecophyto Plan I amounted to EUR 41 million per year, with the remainder going to the Water Agencies.[13] As of 2016, the total amount of tax revenue is expected to reach EUR 150 million, of which EUR 71 million will go to the Ecophyto Plan II. This revenue recycling mechanism, which the FNSEA, among others, lobbied for, was a factor that helped to increase the political acceptability of the tax and subsequent increase in rates.

Between the time the tax was introduced in 2008 and 2013, the annual amount paid by farmers increased by a factor of five (Cour des comptes, 2015). However, farmers' overall contribution to the funding of Water Agencies remains low, in terms of percentage of receipts (6% of all taxes in 2013) and is still well below the health and environmental costs they generate and the incentives they receive (Cour des comptes, 2015; Sainteny, 2011; OECD, 2016). Thus, while the establishment of the tax on diffuse pollution is noteworthy, the polluter pays principle is still not fully applied (Cour des comptes, 2015).

Despite the increases in the tax rate, the tax on diffuse pollution has not been very effective at reducing pesticide use in agriculture (Sainteny, 2011; Lavraut et al., 2013). This is mainly attributed to the relatively low tax rate and the weak price elasticity of demand for pesticides[14] (Dutartre et al., 2014; Carpentier, 2010). To function as an effective incentive to reduce pesticide use, tax rates would need to be raised substantially. Butault et al. (2011) estimated the level of tax that would correspond to reductions in pesticide use. The study modelled the introduction of a tax that would increase the price of pesticides and the resulting impact on various modes of agricultural production. It estimated that to reduce pesticide use by 30%, the tax rate would need to be 100% (of the sale price of the product), while for a reduction of use of 50%, the tax rate would need to be 180%. Thus, moderate increases in the tax rate alone are not sufficient to change behaviour, unless accompanied by other measures such as training, the diffusion of good practices and the development of alternatives (Dutartre et al., 2014; Butault et al., 2011).

Since the last increase in rates in 2011, several proposals have been made to continue to raise the rate and expand the tax base. As part of his efforts to promote agro-ecology, the Minister of Agriculture, requested in 2012 that the ministries of agriculture, environment and finance work together to examine how the revenue from the tax on diffuse pollution could best be used to support actions under the Ecophyto Plan. A joint mission studied ten scenarios to increase the tax rate and/ or enlarge the tax base. The scenario with the highest tax rate was considered to place too high of an economic burden on the agricultural sector.[15] Instead of increasing the tax rate, the government chose to enlarge the tax base to cover a longer list of substances. This decision was the result of political discussions and the final outcome influenced by the fact that the decision to enlarge the tax base could be taken by *décret*, therefore at the initiative of the government, without involving Parliament.[16] In contrast, increasing the tax rate would require legislative action by Parliament.

The change in the tax base took effect on 1 January 2015. It is expected to increase the revenue generated from EUR 41 to 71 million from 2016 (MAAF-MEDDE, 2015). Thus, this choice allowed for an increase in revenue raising, but with tax rates remaining at relatively low levels, the potential incentive effect remain weak.

In a separate development, in 2012, the government eliminated the reduced the rate of the value added tax (VAT) for pesticides and fertilisers via an amendment to the Law of Finance. This amendment followed the publication in 2011 of a comprehensive national study on public subsidies harmful to biodiversity (Sainteny, 2011). The re-establishment of a standard VAT rate on farmers' consumption of fertilisers and pesticides did not have an impact on their production costs, as most farmers are subject to the simplified VAT system and recover VAT that they pay on the purchase of their products. This reform was one of the very few recommendations from the study which was successfully implemented.

3.3. The introduction of a novel instrument: pesticide saving certificates

Despite the numerous actions elaborated under the Plan Ecophyto I, by 2014, the plan had not achieved the desired results to reach the objective of reducing by 50% the use of pesticides ("if possible") between 2008 and 2018 (MAAF-MEDDE, 2015). In light of the disappointing results, a new Ecophyto Plan II was released in 2015. At the same time, strong action was taken to eliminate non-agricultural pesticide use (by municipalities and households) with the adoption of the law on the Energy Transition for Green Growth (*loi de transition énergétique pour la croissance verte*) in 2015.[17]

The Ecophyto Plan II was based on the findings of a mission led by Député Dominique Potier at the request of Prime Minister. The plan maintains the objective of reducing by half the use of pesticides products within 10 years, but postpones the deadline for reaching the objective from 2018 to 2025. The plan sets a short-term goal of a reduction by 25% by 2020 and a 50% reduction by 2025, compared to 2015 (MAAF-MEDDE, 2015). Figure 3.1 depicts the objectives of the first and second Ecophyto Plans plotted against the evolution of pesticide use in agriculture.

Figure 3.1. **Evolution of pesticide use compared to the objectives of the Ecophyto Plans I and II**

Number of unit doses (Nodu)[a] compared to Ecophyto plan targets

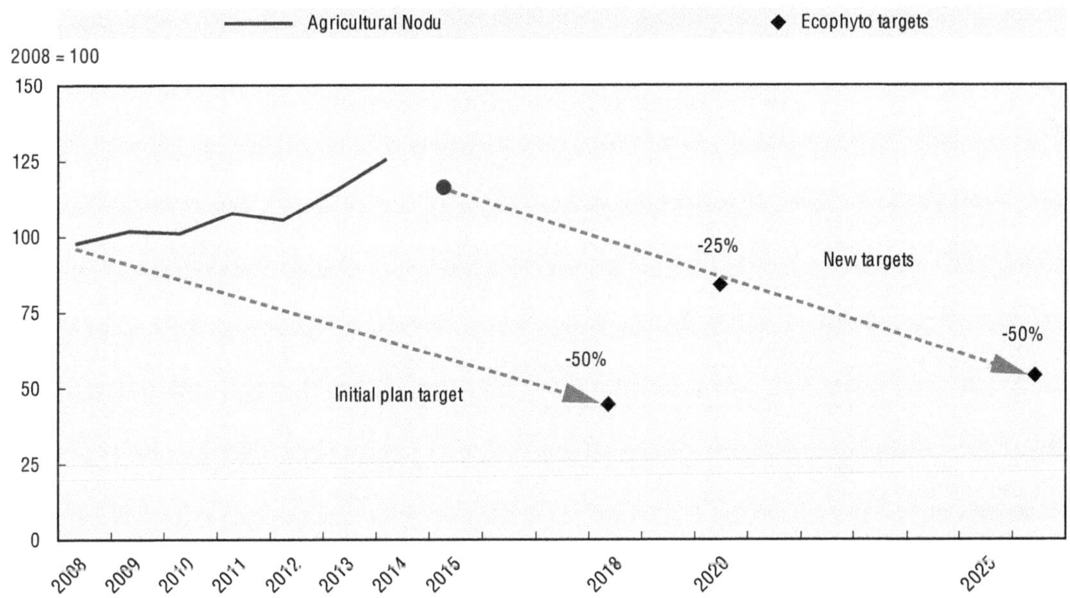

Note: Changes in agricultural "number of unit doses" (Nodu) compared to Ecophyto plan. 2015 is an estimate based on 2012-14 average.

Source: OECD (2016), *OECD Environmental Performance Reviews: France 2016*, OECD Publishing, Paris, *http://dx.doi.org/10.1787/9789264252714-en*. OECD based on data from MAAF (2016), *Tendances du recours aux produits phytopharmaceutiques de 2009 à 2014*.

The preparation of the plan included several studies and consultations to consider the options for introducing changes to existing policies or the introduction of new policy instruments to achieve the plan's goals (Box 3.1). The focus of the new plan is mainly on diffusing and implementing existing techniques for the reduction of pesticide use to as many farmers as possible, along with financial support, while maintaining efforts on research and innovation. Figure 3.2 depicts the evolution of key policies discussed in the case so far.

The establishment of an experimental instrument, the pesticide saving certificates (CEPPs) was recommended by a joint mission consisting of representatives of the General Counsels on agriculture, environment and finance.[18] This mission proposed the CEPPs as an

Box 3.1. **Ecophyto Plan II measures targeting biodiversity**

The Ecophyto Plan II, released in 2015, seeks to address many of the shortcomings of the previous plan. The plan maintains the ambitious target to reduce pesticide use by half within 10 years and includes a number of other measures targeted at benefitting biodiversity. These include:

- A national network monitoring the unintended impacts of agricultural practices on biodiversity. The network is comprised of 500 parcels and focuses on 4 species groups: birds, flora of field edges, beetles and earthworms. The objective is to estimate the impact of agriculture on these species.
- A network of demonstration farms ("DEPHY"), which diffuse information about what is possible in terms of reducing pesticide use, as well as collect agricultural, environmental and economic data.
- An information portal on integrated crop protection.
- Promotion of organic pest control products.

Source: MAAF-MEDDE, 2015.

Figure 3.2. **Evolution of key policies to curb pesticide use in France and presiding governments**

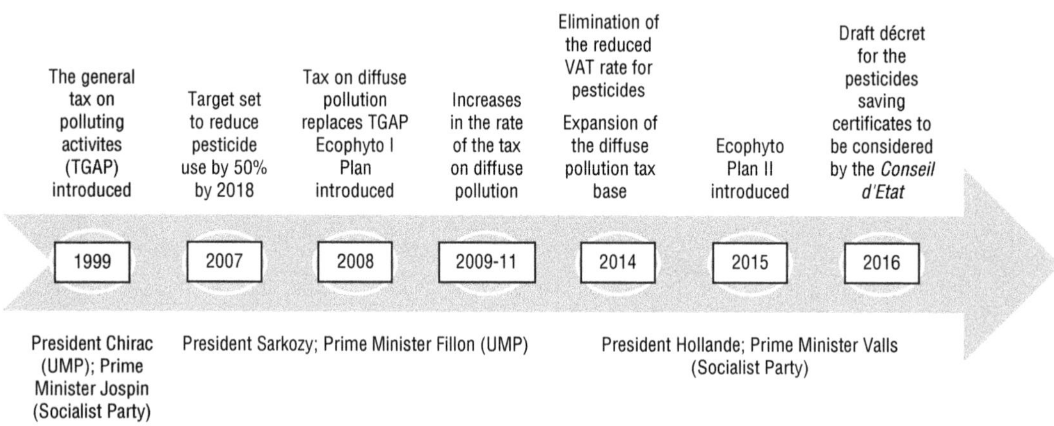

alternative to raising the rate of the diffuse pollution tax or applying more direct regulation (e.g. limiting access to certain products). Barriers to raising tax rates further included limited political acceptability, concerns about potential negative economic impacts on the agricultural sector and concerns that such a rise could inadvertently encourage greater recourse to illegal purchase of pesticides. In addition, the weak price elasticity of pesticide demand was used as an argument against raising rates (Dutartre et al., 2014).

The establishment of CEPPs was included in the Law of the Future of Agriculture and Forestry (*Loi d'Avenir Agricole et Forestiere*) (LAAF) of 2014. Inspired by the energy saving certificates, the CEPPs require pesticide distributors to encourage farmers to adopt practices recognised to be effective in lowering the use of pesticides and the associated risks and impacts. This requires defining a standardised and approved list of actions which reduce pesticide use and quantifying the expected reduction, differentiated by crop type. In exchange for taking these approved actions, the distributors receive CEPPs in accordance with the expected pesticide "savings" achieved. Distributors are expected to develop their role as an advisor and guide in suggesting alternatives to pesticide use as a part of this process. The approach of the scheme is to stimulate the diffusion of good practices in the sector where technical solutions exist, but a number of barriers to implementation remain, such as risk aversion or a poor understanding of the potential benefits for farmers.

The scheme will have an overall target of reducing pesticide use, which will be shared among individual distributors (in a manner that is still to be determined). They will self-report their actions taken under the scheme, with an external audit undertaken for each distributor at least once during the period of experimentation. At the end of the period of experimentation, distributors must demonstrate a reduction of pesticide use compared to a baseline. Distributors who have not met their obligations, either by implementing recognised actions or by purchasing certificates from other obligated parties, will be penalised (MAAF-MEDDE, 2015).

In its recent (2015) recommendation on pesticides, the Green Economy Committee listed a number of necessary conditions that will need to be in place for the good performance of the scheme. Among the long list of conditions cited are: ensuring transparency in the definition of the list of approved actions; vigilance regarding possible leakage (savings generated by adoption of actions offset by increased use of pesticides elsewhere) or double-counting; evaluation and re-adjustment in the course of the period of experimentation; considering the possibility of including seeds treated with pesticides in the scheme; and continued development of indicators which can reliably measure the impact of pesticide use (Green Economy Committee, 2015).

Stakeholder consultations to inform the design of CEPPs

A collaborative approach was taken in the process of developing proposals on the specific design of the CEPPs, including public consultations led by the ministries of environment and agriculture. Inspired by the "Grenelle" model, this consisted on broad engagement with a wide diversity of stakeholders with periodic meetings spanning nearly a year and a half. This approach engaged the vital support of research institutions, including INRA, which contributed to a sound evidence base the government could rely on to defend against lobbying efforts attempting to stall or weaken action on pesticide reduction. It also permitted the engagement of a diversity of actors from the agricultural sector, including those pioneers advocating for stronger action on agro-environmental measures and actively demonstrating the viability of alternative techniques.

Consultations took place in 2014 with professional organisations representing farmers, distributors, as well as scientific and technical experts. The mechanism of pesticide saving certificates faced criticism from agricultural professional organisations, in particular due to the complexity of the scheme, which was described as an "incomprehensible system" ("*usine à gaz*") (Dutartre et al., 2014). The scheme was also criticised for focusing on the reduction in pesticide *use*, rather than the reduction in the *impact* of the pesticide use and thus, the risk related to pesticide use.[19] However, the reduction of pesticide use is the main lever to reduce the risk related to their use. In general, agricultural organisations preferred the CEPPs as a policy option, compared to increasing the tax on pesticides or more direct regulation. The majority of agricultural actors consulted indicated that more direct regulation would not be acceptable (Dutartre et al., 2014).

Distributors raised concerns about possible competitiveness impacts related to the implementation of the CEPPs (Dutartre et al., 2014). As France is the only country in the EU implementing this novel instrument, distributors raised concerns about possible market distortions that it could create for French pesticide distributors. They noted that there could be possible distortions, especially along the border, between French farmers who buy pesticides from French distributors subject to both the tax on diffuse pollution and the CEPP scheme and those who buy pesticides from a (non-French) European distributor not subject to either regime. However, the joint mission concluded that potential competitiveness impacts are not related directly to CEPPs, but instead concern fraudulent behaviour and should be addressed by strengthening existing controls (Dutartre et al., 2014). Furthermore, it is recognised that a reduction in pesticide use can be made while still maintaining production levels, as demonstrated by the DEPHY network[20] (MAAF, 2016b). However, this requires a change in management practices, which take time to diffuse widely.

Drawing on the recommendations of the joint mission, the Ministry of Agriculture set out the detailed design of the CEPPs in an ordonnance and a draft *décret* (an order with legal force issued by the French President or Prime Minister). In the draft *décret*, the Ministry of Agriculture proposed that the CEPPs should target a reduction in pesticide use (as measured by the NODU) of 20% after the 5-year period of experimentation. It was proposed that failure to reach the objective for reduction would be sanctioned by a fine of EUR 11 per NODU of savings lacking, an estimated 11 times the net profit per NODU of pesticide distributors. The proposed overall target of the scheme, the level of the sanction and the indicator to measure progress were all contested by pesticide distributors and the agricultural union, FNSEA.[21] The Ministry of Agriculture agreed to discuss these three points with these stakeholders. Stakeholders argued that the level of the sanction was too high and was not an accurate estimate of distributors' net profit per NODU, but the gross revenue per NODU. Also, they referenced the example of the energy saving certificates, which started with a low level of sanctions that eventually increased as the scheme was refined and improved. As a result of these negotiations with stakeholders, the level of the sanction in the draft *décret* was reduced by more than half, to EUR 5 per NODU.

The indicator to measure progress under the CEPP scheme will remain the NODU. Although an alternative composite indicator to measure the progress of developing and diffusing economically viable alternatives to pesticide use, as proposed by FNSEA, will also be developed jointly by the ministries of agriculture and environment and used as a complementary measure in the context of the Ecophyto Plan II.

In addition to negotiations with targeted stakeholders, a public consultation on the draft *décret* took place in early May 2016. The overall target of reduction in pesticide use by 20% was seen as acceptable. The draft *décret* will also be evaluated to assess the economic impacts on affected businesses (pesticide distributors and farmers). An environmental impact study is not obligatory.

At the same time, there have been several calls to analyse the possibility to strengthen the incentive nature of the diffuse pollution tax (Green Economy Committee, 2015; Potier, 2014). In particular, in 2015, the Green Economy Committee recommended that a study be undertaken to examine this issue, including an analysis of how the revenue raised could be allocated. The committee recommended that two options be examined: using the revenue to sustain the competitiveness of the agricultural sector and using the revenue to support farmers evolving their practices towards a reduction in pesticide use. The potential use of additional revenue from an eventual increase in the tax was a strongly debated issue within the committee, with environmental NGOs insistent that the revenue should benefit only those farmers changing to more ecological practices and opposed to revenue being used to offset any competitiveness impacts on the sector a higher tax could generate.

Overall, both the Ministries of Environment and Agriculture agree that any future increase in the tax on diffuse pollution should be used to support actions to encourage the reduction of pesticides use. However, there has been disagreement in the past about who would receive the revenue and how it would be used: the Ministry of Environment preferring that the revenue continue to be allocated to the Water Agencies and the Ministry of Agriculture preferring that the revenue is directly recycled to the agricultural sector (to the farmers, via the distributors) (Dutrante et al., 2014). Since the adoption of the Ecophyto Plan II, both ministries co-pilot the plan, and have reached agreement on the objectives and means to implement the plan. This co-pilotage is considered an important element of government efforts to encourage the reduction of pesticide use.

3.4. Lessons for addressing barriers to biodiversity policy reform

Revenue recycling helped secure ambitious targets and political acceptability of reforms

This case illustrates a number of challenges in implementing effective biodiversity policy reforms and highlights lessons for overcoming some of them. In this case, the distribution of costs and benefits of policy reforms has been a facilitating factor for gaining political acceptability. In particular, the tax on diffuse pollution has been widely used as an instrument to finance pesticide reduction policy, rather than as an instrument to generate an incentive for the reduction in pesticide use. Recycling the revenue from the tax to fund actions under the Ecophyto Plan (ultimately benefitting farmers) to reduce pesticide use and Water Agency programmes facilitated decisions to increase the tax rate on diffuse pollution over time, which were relatively modest. This revenue recycling was also a critical factor that supported maintaining the ambitious reduction targets under the Ecophyto Plan II. Further, the fact that farmers benefit from a simplified VAT scheme and that the removal of the reduced VAT rate did not affect production costs for most farmers undoubtedly contributed to the acceptance of the removal of this environmentally-harmful subsidy.

However, the low level of the tax on diffuse pollution has not provided an incentive to reduce use and the actions under the Ecophyto Plan I financed by the revenue generated from the tax has fallen well short of the government's own target while pesticide use continues to increase. Substantial increases in the tax rate have not been pursued, primarily due to concerns about negative economic impacts, especially in some farming sectors where alternatives are more limited. Rather than regulating pesticide use more strictly, the government has chosen to work in collaboration with farmers and pesticide distributors to encourage practices that reduce use. Interestingly, future attempts to raise the tax rate on diffuse pollution may be stymied by strong opposing views about how the additional revenue raised should be used: whether allocated to the general budget, to actions by farmers and Water Agencies aimed at improving ecological outcomes or to offset potential competitiveness impacts in the agricultural sector. This topic has already provoked vigorous debate among stakeholders in the Green Economy Committee.

In general, revenue from environmentally related taxes, such as the tax on diffuse pollution, should be treated as general government revenue and used to maintain spending, reduce debt or reduce other taxes (OECD, 2011). While the earmarking of revenues from environmentally related taxes (e.g. to fund spending on pesticide reduction policies) can promote transparency and thus help garner public support and thereby the political acceptability of the tax, it also bypasses or pre-empts the annual budgets, where departments compete for funds on an equal footing, and creates a precedent for other government agencies to have their own earmarked funds (OECD, 2013).

Concerns about competitiveness impacts stalled reforms in some instances

This case also provides an example of how competitiveness concerns have been sufficient to limit the increases in the rate of the tax on diffuse pollution to modest levels, far below levels that could have a strong incentive impact on pesticide use. However, concerns about potential negative impacts on competitiveness have not thwarted the introduction of a novel policy instrument (the CEPPs), despite France being the only EU country to put such an instrument in place.

Considering the strong opposition of the agriculture sector to stricter regulation or a further increase in tax rates on pesticides, the adoption of CEPPs appears to represent a compromise to gain political acceptability of the reform, at least as far as the choice of policy instrument is concerned. Further compromises have been made in key design features of the scheme, such as the level of sanctions to be imposed for non-compliance following consultations with select stakeholders. Although the government has opted to develop a rather complex, novel instrument, it has not given much consideration to potential risk mitigation instruments, such as insurance, to date. This type of policy instrument could help offset potential revenue losses due to declines in the quality or quantity of production arising from reduced pesticide use. Reflections on developing such instruments are mandated under the Ecophyto Plan II, so should provide an opportunity to consider such alternative approaches in the future.

Finally, although often cast as such in policy debates, pesticide use reduction need not be at odds with the competitivity of agricultural firms. As argued by Potier (2014), the results demonstrated by the range of farmers engaged already in reducing pesticide use – from the pioneers of sustainable agriculture to the champions of precision agriculture – show that such systems can deliver economic, environmental and social benefits, without reducing production. Further, the notion of competitivity itself needs to reflect environmental and social externalities of agricultural production (Potier, 2014).

Broad stakeholder engagement helped to gain support of the agricultural sector

The close co-operation between the Ministries of Environment and Agriculture, along with reliance on the "Grenelle model" of broad stakeholder engagement are viewed as key to advancing policies to curb pesticide use. The agriculture sector has significant heterogeneity, which includes a number of smaller, innovative pioneers, which are helping to push the agro-ecology agenda within the sector. Including a very diverse and broad range of actors avoided the process being captured by only a few large lobby groups. Thus, greater representativeness of stakeholders has had a positive influence on policy reforms in this case. In addition, the frequency of periodic meetings, while time consuming and resource intensive, was an important factor in moving the agenda forward with the engagement of and not in opposition to the agricultural sector. Overall, progress has been rather slow and modest, but it is moving in a positive direction.

However, the "Grennillien" approach does not eliminate the diversity of opinions and interests. According to Potier (2014), a major reason for the failure of the Ecophyto plan was that it was built on a fragile consensus. Gaining agreement on issues where there are real or perceived short term losses is especially difficult. In the absence of Grenelle, it is unlikely that French would have adopted such ambitious targets, but achieving these objectives still requires steady political will.

A robust evidence base is critical for standing firm against lobbying pressure

The engagement of research institutions to build a solid evidence base to support policies to reduce pesticide use has been critical to help the government to stand firm against lobbying pressure from vested interests and to convince reluctant actors to engage. Notably, research support from INRA was instrumental in the development of the EcoPhyto Plan II. Further, an independent commission was convened to develop a scientifically-sound list of approved actions for the CEPPs. Ensuring a robust link between the approved actions and actual reductions in pesticide use is essential for the success of the scheme.

Yet, incomplete information on total environmental and health costs to society of the use of pesticides in France impedes a more thorough cost-benefit analysis of pesticide use and a more comprehensive understanding of the distribution of costs and benefits to society. At present, there has been limited economic evaluation of the costs of negative externalities from pesticide use. An economic evaluation on impacts of pesticide use on public health has yet to be undertaken. This requires much better information on the potential risk to health of pesticide use. Such a valuation study would allow for a more complete evaluation of the benefits of pesticide use against the costs and provide comprehensive information to both policy makers and the public. However, as noted in the recommendation on pesticides of the Green Economy Committee, there is sufficient information on the potential risks of pesticide use to promote stronger action. Incomplete information should not be used as a reason to delay action.

Public concern is an increasingly important driver of reform

There are multiple forces influencing the direction and pace of policy reform to reduce pesticide use in France, including growing public concern, media attention, campaigns by NGOs, policy decisions at the EU level, as well as the influence of agricultural lobbies and other vested interests. Views differ as to the relative influence of these factors. Some argue that the obligations stemming from EU Directives and Regulations have been a major driver, while others point to the heightened attention in the media and NGO campaigns, which have contributed to a more aware and knowledgeable general public and more pronounced action at the highest levels of the French government. What is clear is that public opinion, as expressed through their market choices (via demand for organic products, etc.) is an increasingly important driver of reform. Most agree that the trend towards less pesticide use is irreversible and while certain vested interests many aim to slow or stall reforms, the long-term momentum is toward more environmentally sustainable farming practices.

Notes

1. Including insecticides, fungicides and herbicides.
2. In France in 2012, 63.8 Mt of pesticides were sold, 66.7 Mt were sold in 2013 and 75.3 Mt were sold in 2014 (Eurostat, 2016).
3. The indicator used for this measurement is the "Number of Unit Doses" (NODU). It is expressed in quantities of pesticides in terms of the unit doses of active substances applied. It is calculated on an annual basis at national level, but cannot be broken down by culture (Urruty, et al., 2015), nor at a sub-national scale. The NODU is determined based on required declarations of sales of products

covered by the tax on diffuse pollution. It provides a better indication of potential impacts of pesticide use as compared to simply tracking the volume of quantities sold, which does not take into account changes in the efficiency or toxicity of pesticides, such as older products which were used in larger quantities being replaced by products which can be effective at low doses (Marcus and Simon, 2015). Data released by MAAF (2016) account for climatic variations.

4. The risks of pesticide use to the environment vary considerably from one pesticide to another, depending on the intrinsic characteristics of their active ingredients (toxicity, persistence, etc.) and use patterns (applied volumes, application period and method, crop and soil type, etc.).
5. Reviewing a range of studies between 1963 and 1991, Bourguet and Guillemaud (2016) note that a benefit-cost ratio of 4 has become the most widely-cited figure. The benefit-cost ratio reflects the marginal productivity of agriculture due to pesticide use compared to the cost of buying pesticides.
6. These are costs associated with the impact of pesticides on the environment and human health, regulatory measures and defensive behaviour. They are either internal to the market, but "hidden" in the sense that users (e.g., farmers) may not be aware of them, or external to the market.
7. France is the leading agricultural producer in the European Union with production valued at EUR 75 billion in 2013 (MAAF-MEEDE, 2015).
8. They must be certified by the government to provide this advice, which must be based on a risk analysis, propose alternatives to pesticide use and by formally documented and signed by the advisor. The government certified requires an audit every two years.
9. This target exceeds the requirements set out in EU Directives and Regulations on pesticides. While the target was not included in the Grenelle Law I (2009) or II (2010), it was included in a national action plan led by the Ministry of agriculture.
10. More recent manifestations of the "Grenelle model" include a 6th group, Parliamentarians. This is referred to as the "Grenelle + 1" model.
11. It was in the course of the Grenelle negotiations that "if possible" was added to the target for pesticide reduction (Potier, 2014).
12. Notably, nitrogen fertiliser is not covered by this tax, which is paradoxical in view of the objectives of the EU Framework Directives on Water and Nitrates (Cour des comptes, 2015).
13. The Finance Law of 2012 set a EUR 41 million ceiling on the annual contribution from the tax to the Ecophyto plan for the period 2012-18 (Potier, 2014). Potier's mission recommended increasing the contribution of the revenue of the diffuse pollution tax to the Ecophyto plan to EUR 100 million per year.
14. Aubertot et al. (2005) note that the price elasticity of pesticide use is low in the short term, but higher in the longer term. Higher price elasticity in the long term reflects the possibility to adopt the full range of alternatives to pesticide use available to agriculture (Carpentier, 2010).
15. The final report of the joint mission was not released to the public.
16. The possibility to tax a broader range of substances was already included in the LEMA.
17. Non-agricultural use accounts for about 5-10% of all pesticide use in France. The ban for municipal use will take effect at the start of 2017 and the ban for households will take effect in 2019. Infractions can be sanctioned by a prison sentence of up to 6 months with a fine of EUR 30 000 (MEDDE, 2016).
18. Specifically, the General Counsel on Food, Agriculture and Rural Spaces (*Conseil Général de l'Alimentation, de l'Agriculture et des Espaces Ruraux*, CGAAER), the General Counsel on Environment and Sustainable Development (*Conseil Général de l'Environnement et du Développemnt Durable*, CGEDD), and the Inspector General of Finances (*l'Inspection Générale des Finances*, l'IGF).
19. Notably, there is not a simple link between the intensity of pesticide treatment, as measured by the Index of the Frequency of Treatment (IFT) and the impact on the environment, which varies in function with the date of application, the soil type and the toxicity of the product used (Dutartre, 2014).
20. As of 2014, the DEPHY network included 1900 farms using agricultural techniques to reduce pesticide use. The network has shown that it is possible to reduce pesticide use while maintaining productivity levels (MAAF, 2016b).
21. Using the NODU as the key indicator for the Ecophyto Plans has been criticised by representatives of the agricultural sector. They argue that the way it is constructed will tend to show disappointing results despite progress reducing the use of more dangerous products. For example, as more dangerous products are banned and replaced by less concentrated products that require greater doses and more frequent treatment, the result will be an increase in the NODU, even though the risks related to the pesticide use is, in principle, reduced.

References

Aubertot et al. (Eds.) (2005), *Pesticides, agriculture et environnement. Réduire l'utilisation des pesticides et limiter leurs impacts environnementaux,* [Pesticides, Agriculture and the Environment : Reducing the Use of Pesticides and Limiting their Environmental Impact], Collective scientific expertise, synthesis report, INRA et Cemagref.

Beketov, M. et al. (2013), "Pesticides reduce regional biodiversity of stream invertebrates", *Proceedings of the National Academy of Sciences* 110(27): 11039-11043, *www.pnas.org/cgi/doi/10.1073/pnas.1305618110.*

Böcker and Finger (2016), "European pesticide tax schemes in comparison: An analysis of experiences and development", *Sustainability*, 8(378), *http://dx.doi.org/10.3390/su8040378.*

Bommelaer, O. and J. Devaux (2012), "Le financement de la gestion des ressources en eau en France" (actualisation de janvier 2012) [Financing water resources management in France], *Études & documents* n°62, Janvier 2012, Commissariat général au développement durable, La Défense.

Bommelaer, O. and J. Devaux (2011), "Coûts des principales pollutions agricoles de l'eau" [Costs of main agricultural water pollution], *Études et documents*, no. 52, Septembre 2011, Commissariat général au développement durable, [General Commission for Sustainable Development], La Défense.

Bourguet, D. and T. Guillemaud (2016), "The hidden and external costs of pesticide use", *Sustainable Agriculture Reviews*, Sustainable Agriculture Reviews 19, *http://dx.doi.org/10.1007/978-3-319-26777-7_2.*

Butault, J.-P. et al. (2011), "L'utilisation des pesticides en France : état des lieux et perspectives de réduction", *Notes et études socio-économiques* no. 35, October 2011, pp. 7-26, Centre d'Études et de Prospective, Ministère de l'Agriculture, de l'Alimentation, de la Pêche, de la Ruralité et de l'Aménagement du Territoire, *http://agriculture.gouv.fr/lutilisation-des-pesticides-en-france-etat-des-lieux-et-perspectives-de-reduction.*

Cour d'appel of Lyon (2015), *Arret du 10 Septembre 2015*, [Decision of September 10, 2015], Décision du Tribunal de Grande Instance de Lyon, SAS Monsanto Agriculture France v. Monsieur Paul Francois.

Cour des comptes (2015), "Les agences de l'eau et la politique de l'eau : une cohérence à retrouver" [Water agencies and water policy: coherence to be found], in *Rapport public annuel* 2015, Cour des comptes, Paris, *www.ccomptes.fr/Publications/Publications/Rapport-public-annuel-2015.*

Cour des comptes (2013), *Les certificats d'économies d'énergie* [Energy Savings Certificates], Cour des comptes, Paris, *www.ccomptes.fr/Actualites/Archives/Les-certificats-d-economies-d-energie* (accessed 22 March 2016).

Dutartre, S. et al. (2014), *Préfiguration de la mise en œuvre des Certificats d'Économie de Produits Phytosanitaires (CEPP), mission d'appui* [Foreshadowing the Implementation of the Plant Protection Products Saving Certificates Support Mission], un rapport pour l'Inspection Générale des Finances, la Conseil Général de l'Alimentation, de l'Agriculture et des Espaces Ruraux, et le Conseil Général de l'Environnement et du Développement Durable, juillet 2014.

Eurostat, (2016), "Pesticide sales", *http://ec.europa.eu/eurostat/web/products-datasets/-/aei_fm_salpest09* (accessed 27 June 2016).

Geiger, F. et al. (2009), "Persistent negative effects of pesticides on biodiversity and biological control potential on European farmland", *Basic and Applied Ecology*, 11 (2010) 97-105.

Green Economy Committee (*Comité pour l'economie verte*), (2015), "Avis du Comité pour l'economie verte du 16 juillet 2015 portant diagnostic sur les instruments économiques relatifs à l'utilisation des produits phytosanitaires et portant recommendation sur les certificats d'économie de produit phytopharmaceutiques" [Recommendations of the Commission for Green Growth of 16 July 2015 based on the diagnosis of economic instruments relating to pesticide use and the recommendation on plant protection product savings certificates].

Institut de Radioprotection et de Sûreté Nucléaire (ISRN), (2015), "Baromètre" [Barometer], *http://barometre.irsn.fr/* (accessed 27 June 2016).

Levraut, A.-M. et al. (2013), *Évaluation de la politique de l'eau* [Evaluation of Water Policy], an analytical report commissioned by le Conseil général de l'environnement et du développement durable, le Conseil général de l'alimentation, de l'agriculture et des espaces ruraux, le Conseil général de l'Économie, de l'Industrie, de l'Énergie et des Technologies, l'Inspection générale des finances, et l'Inspection générale de l'administration, June 2013.

Ministry of Agriculture, Food and Forests (MAAF) (2016a), *Utilisation des produits phytosanitaires: Résultats nationaux pour l'année 2014 et lancement du nouveau plan Ecophyto II* [Use of plant protection production : national results for the year 2014], Press release, March 8, 2016.

Ministry of Agriculture, Agrifood and Forestry (MAAF) (2016b), *Ecophyto, Note de suivi 2015, Tendances du recours aux produits phytopharmaceutiques de 2009 à 2014,* [Ecophyto Tracking Note 2015, Trends in the Use of Pesticides from 2009 to 2014].

Ministry of Agriculture, Food and Forests and Ministry of Ecology and Sustainable Development (MAAF-MEDDE) (2015), *Plan Ecophyto II,* [Plan Ecophyto II] Ministère de l'Agriculture de l'Agroalimentaire et de la Forêt, Ministère de l'Écologie, du Développement durable et de l'Énergie, Paris, *http://agriculture.gouv.fr/sites/minagri/files/151022_ecophyto.pdf.*

Ministry of Ecology and Sustainable Development (MEDDE) (2016), "Les pesticides interdits dans les espaces verts en 2017 et les jardins en 2019" [Pesticides Banned in Green Spaces in 2017 and in Gardens in 2019"], *www.developpement-durable.gouv.fr/Les-pesticides-interdits-dans-les,39463.html* (accessed 18 July 2016).

Marcus, V. and O. Simon (2015), "Les pollutions par les engrais azotés et les produits phytosanitaires : coûts et solutions" [Pollution from nitrogen fertilisers and plant protection products: Costs and solutions], *Études et documents*, n° 136, Commissariat général au développement durable.

Observatoire des Résidu de Pesticides (ORP) (2015) "Qu'est-ce que la TGAP?" [What is the TGAP ?], *www.observatoire-pesticides.gouv.fr/index.php?pageid=184&ongletlstid=165&locator=Foire%20aux%20 questions* (accessed 9 February 2016).

OECD (2016), *OECD Environmental Performance Reviews: France 2016*, OECD Publishing, Paris, *http:// dx.doi.org/10.1787/9789264252714-en.*

OECD (2012), *Water Quality and Agriculture: Meeting the Policy Challenge*, OECD Publishing, Paris, *http:// dx.doi.org/10.1787/9789264168060-9-en.*

OECD (2011), "Environmental taxation: A guide for policy makers", *www.oecd.org/env/tools-evaluation/ 48164926.pdf* (accessed 29 June 2016).

Poláková, J. et al. (2011), *Addressing Biodiversity and Habitat Preservation through Measures Applied under the Common Agricultural Policy*, Report Prepared for DG Agriculture and Rural Development, Contract No. 30-CE- 0388497/00-44, Institute for European Environmental Policy, London.

Potier, D. (2014), "Pesticides et agro-écologie: les champs du possible" [Pesticides and agro-ecology : the range of possibilities], Rapport de Dominique Potier, Député de Meurthe et Moselle, au Premier Ministre Manuel Valls, [Report from Dominique Poteir, deputy of Meurthe et Moselle to the Prime Minister Manuel Valls], November 2014, Paris, *www.dominiquepotier.com/UserFiles/File/rapport-dpotier-pesticides-et-agro-ecologie-basse-def.pdf* (accessed 14 March 2016).

Saint-Ges, V. and M.-C. Belis-Bergouignan (2009), "Ways of reducing pesticides use in Bordeaux vineyards", *Journal of Cleaner Production*, Vol. 17, pp. 1644-1653.

Sainteny, G. (2011), "Public incentives harmful to biodiversity", Report of the commission chaired by Guillaume Sainteny, Centre d'analyse stratégique.

Skevas, T. et al. (2013), "Designing the emerging EU pesticide policy: A literature review", *Wageningen Journal of Life Sciences*, 64-65, pp. 95-103.

SOes (2016), "Les pesticides dans les eaux" [Pesticides in water], *www.statistiques.developpement-durable.gouv.fr/lessentiel/s/pesticides-eaux.html* (27 June 2016).

Trasande, L. et al. (2015), "Estimating burden and disease costs of exposure to endocrine-disrupting chemicals in the European Union", *Journal of Clinical Endocrinology and Metabolism*, 100(4): pp. 1245-1255, *http://dx.doi.org/10.1210/jc.2014-4324.*

Urruty et al. (2015), "Usage des pesticides en agriculture: effets des changements d'usage des sols sur les variations de l'indicateur NODU" [Pesticide use in agriculture : impact of the change in land use on the variations of the NODU indicator], *http://agriculture.gouv.fr/usage-des-pesticides-en-agriculture-effets-des-changements-dusage-des-sols-sur-les-variations-de* (accessed 24 February 2016).

ANNEX 3.A1

Pesticide taxes in selected countries

Table 3.A1.1. **Pesticide taxes in selected countries**

Country	Tax base	Tax rate(s)	Imposition point	Year introduced	Other details (earmarking, exemptions, total revenue)
Denmark	Active ingredients in pesticides. Revised in 2013 into a more differentiated tax scheme	Insecticides: 54% of retail price Herbicides, fungicides, growth regulators: 34% of retail price Wood preservatives: 3% of gross value	Wholesalers/importers	1996	Earmarking: 100% for environmental purposes and to compensate farmers. Total revenue in 2013 DKK 659 million (~EUR 88.4 million)
France	Pesticides (differentiated by category of substance)	Substances which are very toxic, toxic, carcinogenic, mutagenic or toxic to reproduction: EUR 5.1/ tonne Substances which are hazardous for the environment: EUR 2/ tonne Mineral chemicals which are hazardous for the environment: EUR 0.9/ tonne	Pesticide distributors	1999 (TGAP) replaced by current tax in 2008	Tax revenue used to finance the Ecophyto Plans I and II, with the remainder going to the Water Agencies.
Norway	Pesticides (differentiated tax scheme)	Banded tax system, with rates determined by a complex formula	Industry, importers/wholesalers	1988	Estimated revenue in 2015 NOK 50 million (~EUR 5.8 million)
Sweden	Pesticides (fixed tax scheme)	EUR 3.64 per kilogramme of active substance	Wholesalers/importers	1984	Exemptions: Wood preservatives. Total revenue in 2015 SEK 70 million (~ EUR 7.5 million)
United States (Washington State)	Pesticides	0.7% of wholesale value			Earmarking: 100% funds are distributed to the Department of Ecology to help clean up and manage solid and hazardous waste in the state of Washington.

Source: OECD (2016), *Database on instruments used for environmental policy*; Böcker and Finger (2016); Skevas et al. (2013).

Chapter 4

Agricultural subsidy reform in Switzerland

This chapter analyses the reform of agricultural subsidies in the Swiss Agricultural Policy 2014-17. From a political economy perspective, it examines how the direct payments system for farmers was reformed to better target policy objectives, including for biodiversity. The case study draws lessons learned for overcoming barriers to reform, including the importance of seizing windows of opportunity, building an alliance of economic and ecological interests, engaging a broad range of stakeholders and devising politically and socially acceptable compromises, including the use of transition payments to offset negative distributional impacts.

Introduction

Since the early 1990s, Switzerland has undertaken a series of major agricultural policy reforms, reducing market intervention and introducing the system of direct payments, which included both general direct payments and ecological payments. However, by 2009, many of the ecological targets had not been achieved and more fundamental questions were being raised about the effectiveness and efficiency of the direct payments system. This led to the reform of the direct payments system to better target policy objectives, including for biodiversity.

This case study[1] examines the political economy aspects of the reform of the direct payments system adopted under the Agricultural Policy 2014-17. It demonstrates how an alliance of market-oriented and ecological interests can help to spur reform and how windows of opportunity can create conditions conducive to reform. Broad stakeholder engagement allowed for the inclusion of smaller groups, which could better express the diverse interests of the agricultural sector, including those who stood to benefit from the reform. The case also illustrates how devising politically and socially acceptable compromises, including the use of transition payments to offset negative distributional impacts, can help overcome barriers to reform.

4.1. The impact of agriculture on biodiversity in Switzerland

From an economic perspective, agriculture plays a relatively minor and declining role in Switzerland. Its share of gross domestic product (GDP) is less than 0.7% (Jarrett and Moeser 2013) and the share of employment is around 4%. A decline in agricultural area (i.e. 5.4% between 1985 and 2009[2]) has been mainly due to increased urbanisation and to land abandonment, as well as to increased forest coverage (FOAG, 2015). Agriculture is nevertheless the largest user of land in Switzerland (Environment Switzerland, 2015), with more than one third of overall area used for this purpose (23.4% agricultural areas and 12.4% alpine agricultural areas [FOAG, ed., 2015])[3] and therefore plays a crucial role for biodiversity.

Switzerland is characterised by a high diversity of natural habitats. This is due in part to the topographic and climatic variability and the diversity of bedrock and soil properties. It is also due to human activity, particularly in mountainous regions where traditional extensive agricultural practices have created a variety of microstructures (e.g. dry stone walls) and biotopes[4] (e.g. hay meadows) that provide habitats for many species (FOAG, 2015). In general, diverse agricultural practices and ecosystems contribute to more diverse agro-ecosystems.

According to Switzerland's 5th National Report under the Convention on Biological Diversity however, biodiversity is in an unsatisfactory state (FOEN, 2014). Given the various pressures, almost half (47%) of all 160 types of habitats are threatened according to the Red List (predominantly water-bodies, wetlands, and uncultivated open land of agro-ecosystems and settlements). A further 16% of the habitats are classified as near threatened. Moreover, 36% of known species in Switzerland are categorised as threatened (Figure 4.1).

Figure 4.1. **Threatened species according to the Red List**

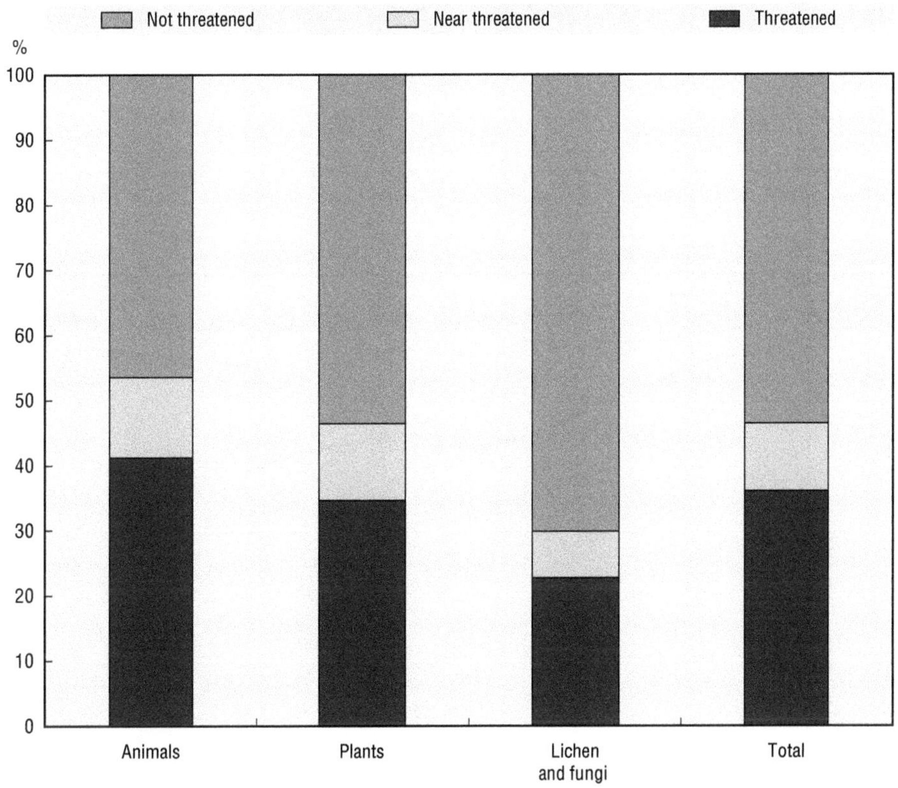

Note: Up until 2012, 10 350 species (a quarter of the 45 890 known species) had been evaluated. Of those evaluated, there were 3 109 animal species, 3 572 plant species and 3 669 lichen and fungi (FOEN, 2014).
Source: Data from FOEN, 2014.

The main drivers of biodiversity loss are changes in land and water use and management and pollution.[5] Most habitats are under intense pressure. They are also disappearing, particularly in agricultural areas, where areas used for settlement (e.g. construction for housing) and transport are spreading and land use is becoming more and more intensive[6] (FOEN, 2014). Settlement areas and infrastructure facilities fragment the landscape, isolating stocks of species. The improper use of fertilisers and pesticides and unsuitable management methods can have an extensive environmental impact (Environment Switzerland, 2015). The external costs of pesticides have been estimated at CHF 100 million (Zandonella et al., 2014). Moreover, nitrogen levels in 95% of forest area exceed the critical load limits as well as 100% of the raised bogs, 84% of the lowland moors and 42% of species-rich dry meadows. This is due to ammonia from agriculture and combustion gases from motorised transport (Environment Switzerland, 2015). Invasive alien species and climate change pose an additional threat to many native species and ecosystems (FOEN, 2014).

Over the past decades, the environmental performance of Swiss agriculture has generally improved. Reforms in the 1990s reduced nutrient surpluses and greenhouse gas emissions, but later reforms reversed these trends due to a policy-induced expansion of the livestock sector.[7] Environmental cross-compliance[8] has had a positive effect on farmland biodiversity, while contributing to the reduced nitrate leaching and phosphorus pollution of surface water (Figure 4.2). Despite improvements, environmental challenges, such as surface and groundwater pollution from pesticides and nutrients, remain (OECD, 2015a).

Figure 4.2. **Development of key agri-environmental indicators in Switzerland, 1990-2010**

Index 1990 = 100

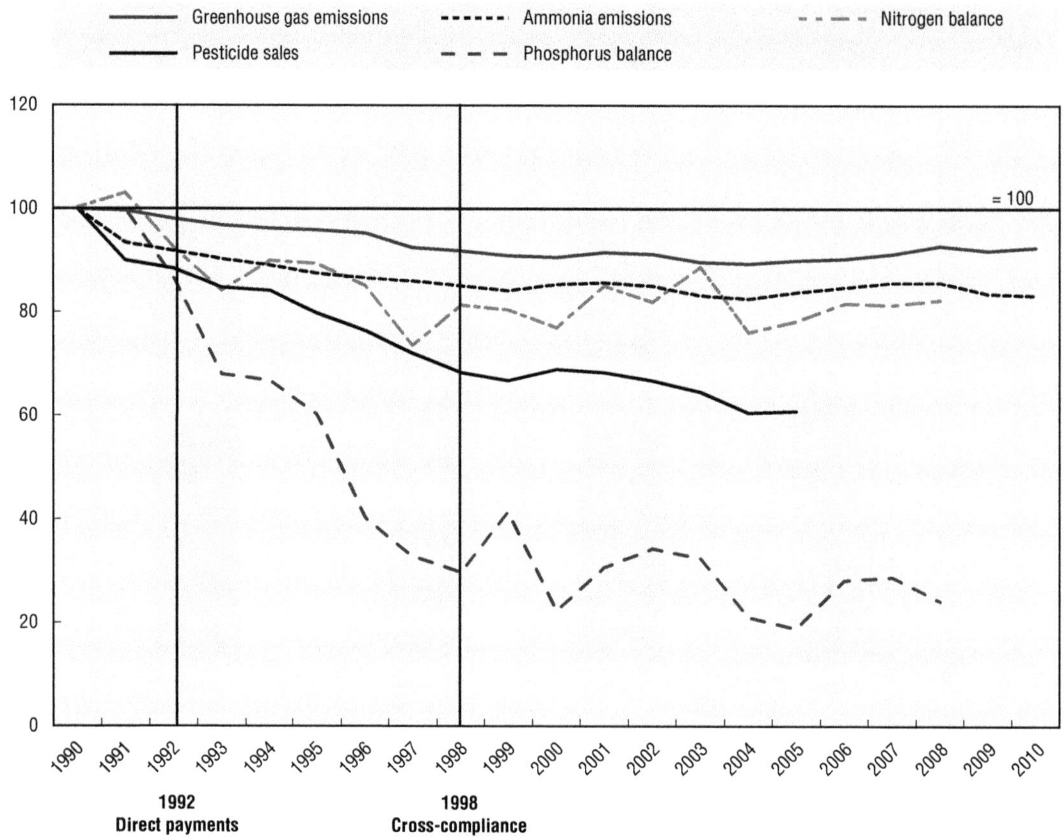

Source: OECD (2013), *OECD Compendium of Agri-environmental Indicators.*

Ecosystems provide a number of services, many of which are also essential for agriculture.[9] These include pollination, biological pest control and the formation and conservation of fertile soils. For example, Besser (2010) estimated that on average, Swiss bee colonies provided a yearly agricultural production worth about CHF 256 million (USD 213 million) due to pollination services, over the period 1997 to 2006. Biodiversity in the soil ensures fertile soils, in which organic waste materials are transformed into simpler inorganic components which are then supplied to plants as food. The genetic diversity in livestock breeds and crops, as well as in the wild species related to them, offer the possibility of adapting future agricultural production to different market, production and environmental conditions (Environment Switzerland, 2015). Recent studies have found positive effects of certain Swiss agri-environmental schemes, such as wildflower strips, on natural pest control and crop yield (Tschumi et al., 2016; Tschumi et al., 2015).

Overall, the agricultural sector is perceived as an important element in maintaining food security, and as a provider of positive externalities[10] such as environmental benefits and maintenance of cultural landscapes, which are highly valued by Swiss society (OECD, 2015a). The Federal Constitution specifies that the Confederation shall ensure that agriculture makes a substantial contribution to secure provisioning of the population, to the conservation of natural resources and maintenance of the rural landscape as well as to the decentralisation of the country (see Section 4.2). The importance of sustainable natural resource use in the context of agriculture is also highlighted in the Swiss Biodiversity Strategy (Box 4.1).

Box 4.1. The Swiss Biodiversity Strategy and agriculture

The Swiss Biodiversity Strategy (FOEN, 2012) includes the following overarching goal, with specific reference to agriculture as indicated below.

1. By 2020, the use of natural resources and interventions involving them are sustainable so that the conservation of ecosystems and their services and of species and their genetic diversity is ensured.

Specific agricultural goal in the Swiss Biodiversity Strategy

"The fulfilment of the "Environmental Targets for Agriculture" (*Umweltziele Landwirtschaft*) is essential for the conservation of biodiversity. The environmental targets shall be implemented on a regionally quantified, qualified and co-ordinated basis in the area of biodiversity. The importance of ecosystem services for agriculture shall be recognised and their valorisation through the market and society shall be guaranteed in the different agricultural production processes. The incentives provided for services for the promotion of biodiversity shall be increased and the quality and interconnection of existing ecological compensation areas shall be improved; new biodiversity priority areas (ecological compensation areas) shall be created where necessary."

The "Environmental Targets for Agriculture" were published by the Federal Office for the Environment (FOEN) and the Federal Office for Agriculture (FOAG) in 2008. They provide the basis for the definition of measures for the conservation and promotion of biodiversity in agricultural areas. Specific goals are set out related to thematic areas, including biodiversity and landscape; climate and air; water; and soil. An assessment of these targets was released in 2013 (Walter et al., 2013). The Federal Authorities are still developing the Biodiversity Action Pan, initially due by mid-2014.

Source: FOEN, 2012; BAFU and BLW, 2008.

4.2. The system of direct payments to agriculture in Switzerland

Key milestones in the evolution of agricultural policy in Switzerland related to environmental objectives

Since the early 1990s, Switzerland has undertaken a series of major agricultural policy reforms. Prior to this, agricultural policy guaranteed farmers fixed prices and markets, an approach that was reaching its limits. The cost to the public budget was rising and the adverse ecological impacts of this production-based approach were becoming more obvious (FOAG, 2004), resulting in negative publicity for the agricultural sector (FOAG, n.d.). At the same time, the General Agreement on Tariffs and Trade (GATT) Uruguay Round of negotiations was increasing pressure to reduce protectionist measures (FOAG, 2004). The reforms have gradually reduced overall levels of support and shifted from market price support[11] to direct payments independent of production volume, that aim to compensate farmers for public and ecological services (Lanz, 2012; FOAG, 2004).[12] Key milestones in the evolution of agriculture policy in Switzerland are summarised in Table 4.1.

Major agricultural policy reform began in 1993. Reforms reduced market intervention, and introduced the system of direct payments. They prepared the way for implementing the

Table 4.1. **Milestones in the evolution of agricultural policy in Switzerland (1990-2016)**

1993	Major agricultural policy reforms began, introducing the system of direct payments. Reforms prepared the way for implementing the consequences of the GATT Agreement in 1994.
1994	Conclusion of the GATT Uruguay Round
9 June 1996	Article 104 of the Federal Constitution approved by voters.
1 January 1999	New Agricultural Act, based on Article 104, came into force, replacing law from 1951
2001	Ordinance on Eco-Quality came into force, introducing financial incentives to improve the quality of certain ecological areas and linking them up to form a network.
2002	Agricultural trade agreement with EU came into force.
May 2009	Extensive review of the effectiveness and efficiency of the direct payments system to reach ecological targets set by the Federal Council.
March 2013	The National Council and Swiss Parliament approve the new Agricultural Policy 2014-17.
2014-present	New Agricultural Policy 2014-17 in force.

Source: Lanz, 2012; FOAG, 2004; FOAG, n.d.

results of the GATT Agreement in 1994 (FOAG, 2004). The most important change related to the system of direct payments in 1993 was the introduction of two main categories of new payments: 1) general direct payments[13] and 2) ecological direct payments (OECD, 2015a). Ecological direct payments were designed to provide incentives for more sustainable use of resources and to reduce pollution, as well as to provide additional compensation to farmers for delivering non-marketed goods and services, such as biodiversity, landscape, and animal welfare. Under the ecological direct payments, farmers could also receive payments for extensive crop production (no use of fungicides, insecticides or plant growth regulators, although fertilisers and herbicides were not restricted) or organic production, which in addition to requirements for extensive production, does not allow use of synthetic pesticides or fertilisers) (Finger and Lehmann, 2012). Participation in these programmes is voluntary (OECD, 2015a).

On June 9, 1996, over 75% of voters approved Article 104 on agriculture to be added to the Federal Constitution (FOAG, 2004). Article 104 enshrined the basic principle of the multi-functionality of agriculture, defining four main tasks of Swiss agriculture: ensure food supplies; production methods should ensure future generations will have fertile soil and clean drinking water (ecological); take care of the landscape; and maintain rural areas (FOAG, 2004). This provided the basis for further agricultural policy reforms.

The new Agricultural Act, which came into force 1 January 1999, replaced the previous 1951 law. Based on Article 104, it introduced major changes, including abolishing or phasing out price and market guarantees which had formed the cornerstone of Swiss agricultural policy since World War II (FOAG, n.d.). The Act also made direct payments conditional on "proof of ecological performance" (Box 4.2), which had previously been voluntary (FOAG, n.d.).

By 2009, however, many of the ecological targets set by the Federal Council[14] on the basis of Article 104 had not been achieved. At the same time, more fundamental questions were being raised, by both farmers and economists, about the effectiveness and efficiency of the direct payments system. This led Parliament to adopt a motion to mandate the Federal Council to review the direct payments system, which culminated in an influential report released on 6 May 2009 entitled *Weiterentwicklung des Direktzahlungssystems* [Further Development of the Direct Payments System], (referred to as WDZ 2009). This review lead to recommendations to better target the direct payments system in the 2014-17 Agricultural Policy (AP 2014-17) (further discussed in Section 3).

Box 4.2. **Proof of ecological performance in Switzerland**

Since 1999, direct payments are conditional on good environmental practices required by "proof of ecological performance" (PEP) and the provision of public goods. Similar to cross-compliance under the EU Common Agricultural Policy (CAP), Swiss direct payments are, however, subject to stricter conditionality than in many other OECD countries (Jarrett and Moeser, 2013; Aviron et al., 2008). Nearly all Swiss farms currently fulfil PEP requirements.

PEP is based on the approach of "integrated production principles". They include:

- **Balanced nutrient use:** maximum 10% surplus of nitrogen and phosphorus as shown by farm's nutrient balance (based on crop requirements)
- **Strict crop rotation:** to reduce the vulnerability of crops to disease and consequently, the need for pesticides.
- **Soil protection:** land must be planted the whole year round whenever possible to reduce the risk of erosion.
- **Minimum share (at least 7%)** of farm's utilised agricultural area must be allocated as **ecological compensation areas (ECAs).** ECAs protect and restore ecosystems close to their natural state. The use of artificial fertilisers and pesticides is very restricted.
- **Animal welfare:** farm animals have to be kept according to legal requirements (including compliance with the animal protection ordinance).
- **Selected and targeted application of pesticides:** restrictions on the timing and use of certain pesticides, consideration of early warning systems and pest forecasts, frequent tests of sprayers.

Ecological cross compliance has been shown to promote biodiversity on grassland and arable land in Switzerland, with measurable benefits for flora, butterflies, ground beetles and spiders (Aviron et al., 2008). However, cross compliance is not sufficient to protect uncommon or endangered species (Aviron et al., 2008; Loser, 2010).

Although there has been a considerable increase in the proportion of land reserved as ECAs, ensuring that their quality and location are sufficient to achieve the desired benefits for biodiversity has been a persistent challenge. In 2001, the Ordinance on Eco-Quality was enacted with the aim to address this issue by introduced financial incentives aimed at improving the quality of certain ecological areas and linking them up to form a network (FOAG, 2004).

Source: FOEN, 2016; OECD, 2015a; Jarrett and Moeser, 2013; FOAG, n.d.; Loser, 2010; Aviron et al., 2008.

The evolution of agricultural support prior to the AP 2014-17

The OECD estimates the total level of support to agriculture in OECD countries by applying the methodology of Producer Support Estimate (PSE). Figure 4.3 shows the trend in total PSE in Switzerland over the past three decades. It illustrates the decline in market price support along with a rise and subsequent stabilisation of direct payments since reforms began in the 1990s. Figure 4.4 illustrates the shifting composition of direct payments over time, with a notable increase in ecological direct payments.

As of 2013, 20% of direct payments were dedicated to achieving environmental protection and animal welfare, with the rest as "general" direct payments (Jarrett and Moeser, 2013). Total ecological direct payments amounted to CHF 645 million, with the largest share (CHF 166 million) going to the category "regularly keeping animals outdoors" (OECD, 2015a).[15]

Figure 4.3. **Declining market support and increasing direct payments in the total Producer Support Estimate, 1986-2015**

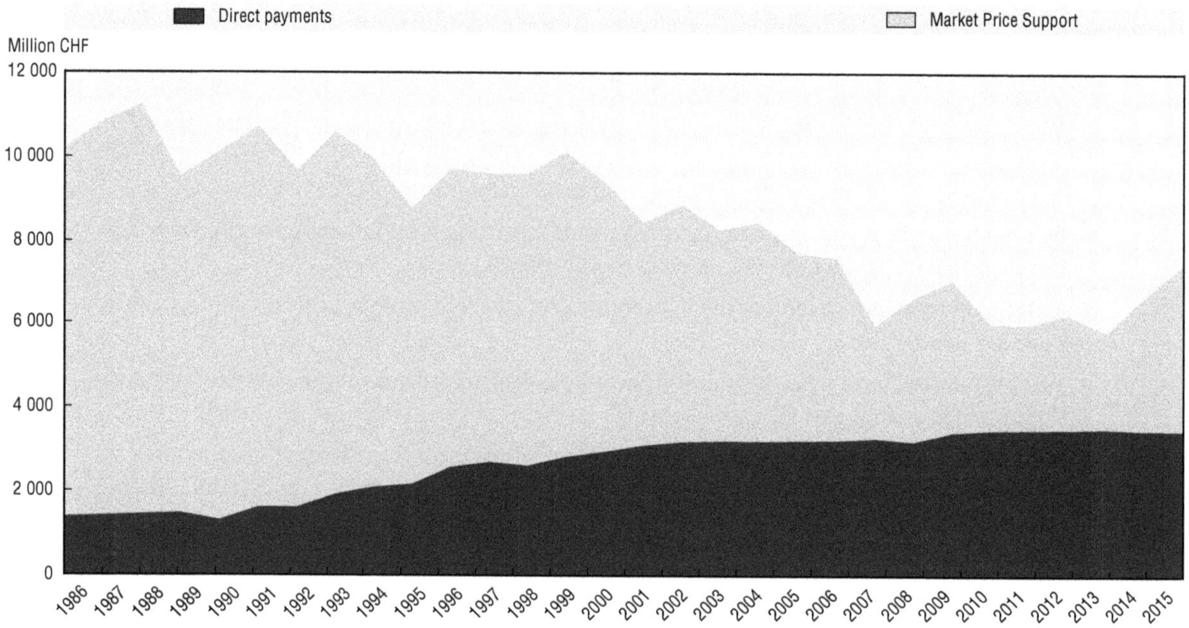

Source: Updated from OECD (2015), *Agricultural Policy Review: Switzerland* (based on data from OECD Agriculture statistics database).

Figure 4.4. **Structure of direct payments, 1986-2013**

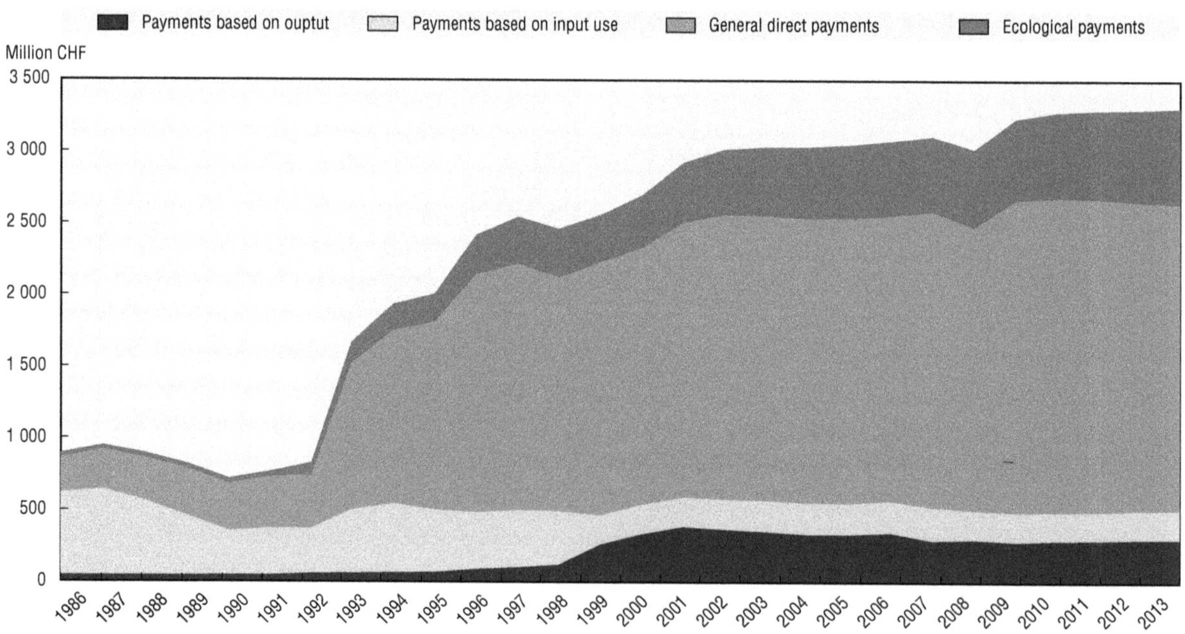

Source: Updated from OECD (2015), *Agricultural Policy Review: Switzerland* (based on data from OECD Agriculture statistics database).

Over the past two decades, the total hectares designated as ecological compensation areas has steadily increased. According to FOAG data, by 2014, over 150 000 hectares were eligible for subsidies, accounting for 14.6% of the utilised agricultural area (Figure 4.5)

Although agricultural support has been reduced since reform began in 1993, levels remain high compared to other OECD countries (Jarrett and Moeser, 2013) (Figure 4.6). As of

Figure 4.5. **Increase in ecological compensation areas, 1996-2014**

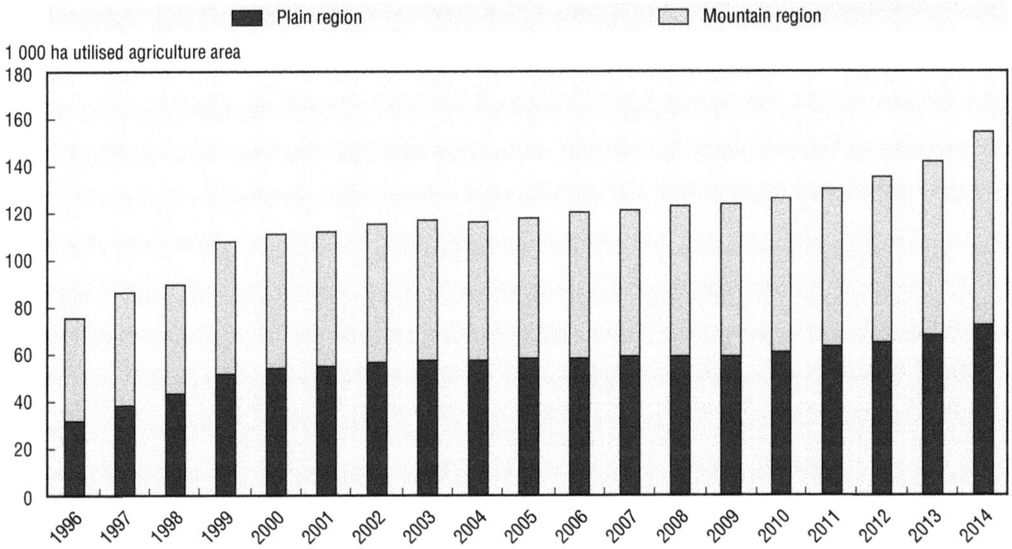

Source: Based on data from FOAG.

Figure 4.6. **Level of composition of agricultural producer support, OECD countries, 1995-2011**

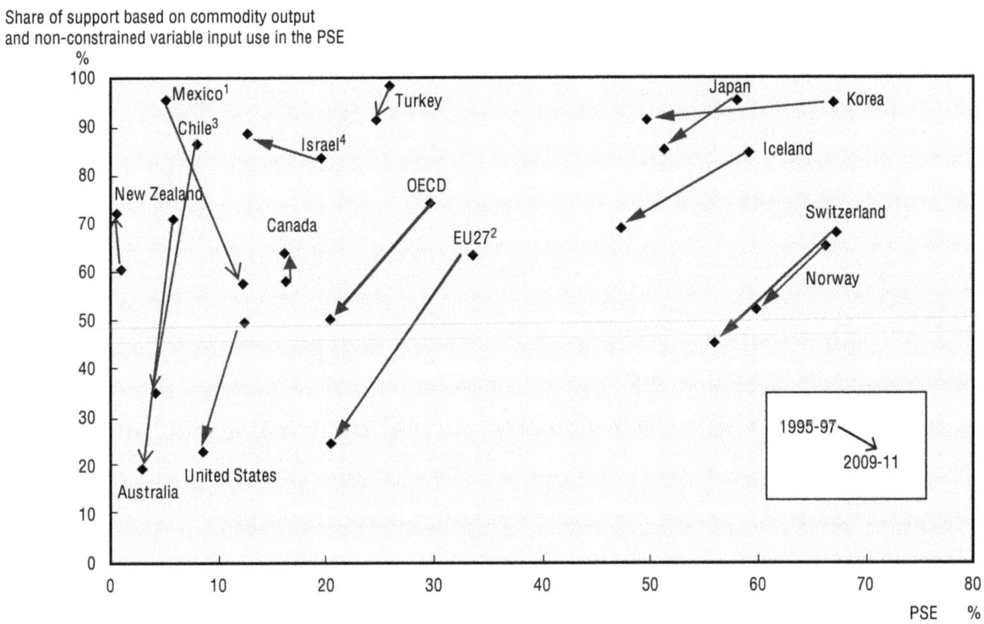

Notes: Producer Support Estimate (PSE): the annual monetary value of gross transfers from consumers and taxpayers to agricultural producers, measured at the arising farm gate level, from policy measures that support agriculture, regardless of their nature, objectives or impacts on farm production or income.

The level of support is presented by the percentage PSE. The composition of support is presented by the share in gross farm receipts of the most production and trade distorting support, including Market Price Support, Payments based on output and Payments based on non-constrained variable input use.

1. For Mexico, the change is measured between 1996-98 and 2009-11.
2. EU15 for 1995-2003; EU25 for 2004-06 and EU27 from 2007.
3. For Chile, change is measured between 1997-99 and 2009-11.
4. For Israel, change is measured between 1997-99 and 2009-11. The statistical data for Israel are supplied by and under the responsibility of the relevant Israeli authorities. The use of such data by the OECD is without prejudice to the status of the Golan Heights, East Jerusalem and Israeli settlements in the West Bank under the terms of international law.

Source: OECD (2015), *OECD Compendium of Agri-environmental Indicators* (based on data from OECD Agriculture statistics database).

2015, direct payments still represented nearly two-thirds of the agricultural contribution (0.7%) to the Swiss GDP (CHF 648 billion), leaving just one third from valued-added (OECD, 2015b). Producer support accounted for more than half of gross farm receipts in 2012 (57%; compared to 18% on average in OECD and less than 4% for Australia, Chile and New Zealand) (Jarrett and Moeser, 2013). For the period 2014-17, a total of CHF 13.83 billion was earmarked for agricultural policy measures, which corresponds to a slightly higher level of annual funding of previous years (Jarrett and Moeser, 2013).

4.3. Reform of direct payments to agriculture in the AP 2014-17

As noted above, Parliamentary debate in 2009 regarding the agricultural policy was fuelled by doubts among both farmers and economists about the effectiveness and efficiency of the existing direct payments system. Simonetta Sommaruga, member of Parliament at the time, called for the motion which was adopted by Parliament to mandate the Federal Council to undertake an extensive review of the system. The Federal Council therefore requested that FOAG undertake a detailed review of the direct payments system with the aim to shape the next series of reforms.

The resulting report, referred to as WDZ 2009, was submitted to Parliament on 6 May 2009. It found that many targets set out by the Federal Council on the basis of Article 104 of the Federal Constitution had not been achieved. Further, the report analysed the relevant internal and external political conditions and developments and defined criteria for an effective and efficient system of direct payments. A central aspect of the report was the description of each of the public services that agriculture should provide and the elaboration of specific targets for each of these services. As a result of this report and subsequent debate, the Parliament's Committee for Economic Affairs and Taxation approved a motion[16] on 16 October 2009 mandating the Federal Council to produce a concrete bill for a revised direct payments system before the end of 2011 (FOAG, 2009).

Ex-ante impact assessment and stakeholder consultations of the AP 2014-17 proposal

A draft proposal of the new policy was prepared and submitted to a broad consultation process involving a wide range of stakeholders, which took place in the spring of 2011. Key players included the Farmers' Union; economics-oriented institutions, such as economiesuisse, in addition to a number of environmental NGOs, such as Agrarallianz,[17] WWF, ProNatura and Birdlife International. These various interests expressed divergent views on the relative importance of objectives relating to security of food supply, trade liberalisation, environmental performance, and landscape cultivation. A Working Group focused on the AP 2014-17 and involving all stakeholders was also established by the Federal Council. Led by FOAG, inter-ministerial consultations also took place in the course of the preparation of the proposed reform.

The draft proposal for the new policy also underwent two rounds of *ex-ante* impact assessment to examine the impacts of the proposed policy changes. The modelling analysis examined the environmental and biodiversity implications of AP 2014-17, as well as those on production and income (Zimmermann et al., 2011 and 2012; FOAG, 2012b) (Box 4.3).

Following the consultations and modelling analysis, the revised proposal was consolidated by the Federal Council and transmitted as a message (*"Botschaft"* or *Message du Conseil Fédéral*) on the AP 2014-17 on 1 February 2012. At the heart of the reform was the further development of the direct payments system by eliminating general payments[18]

Box 4.3. **Findings from the modelling analysis of the proposed AP 2014-17**

To assess the impact of the AP 2014-17 on agriculture, the government requested Agroscope Reckenholz-Tänikon to undertaken modelling analysis.

In a first assessment (Zimmerman et al., 2011), two scenarios were modelled:

- the reference scenario (business as usual)
- the implementation of the Federal Council proposals as part of the message on the AP 2014-17 scenario (dotted line labelled "AP 2014-17" in Figure 4.7).

Results showed that under the AP 2014-17, farm incomes would increase by about 13% above current levels (about 6 percentage points higher than under the reference scenario). Ecological compensation areas would also increase by 13% compared to the current situation and livestock numbers would fall by close to 10%, lowering excess nitrates and phosphates and greenhouse gases as well as improving the impact on biodiversity.

In a subsequent study (Zimmermann, 2012), two additional scenarios were modelled:

- Production scenario: Adaptation of the AP 2014-17 scenario in the direction of farmers' demands, such as an increase in contributions to secure supply (i.e., the *Versorgungssicherheitsbeiträge* – VSB) by one-third, and a simultaneous increase in ecologically-oriented instruments/ biodiversity contributions, production system contributions and resource efficiency contributions.

Figure 4.7. **Modelling results of the impact of AP 2014-17 proposals**

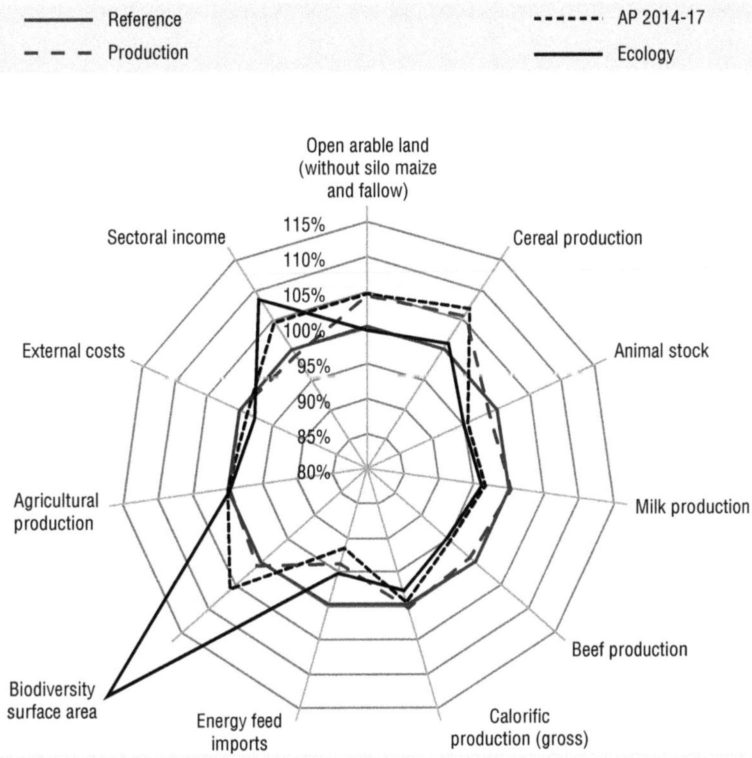

Source: Zimmermann, 2012.

Box 4.3. **Findings from the modelling analysis of the proposed AP 2014-17** *(cont.)*

- Ecology scenario: Adaptation of the AP 2014-17 scenario in the direction of demands from conservation groups and the retail trade: i.e., reduction in contributions to secure supply by one-third with equivalent increase in contributions to ecologically orientated instruments, production system contributions and resource efficiency contributions.

The results showed that the AP 2014-17 scenario was better than the business as usual scenario across nearly all indicators. Also, for most indicators, results for the AP 2014-17 fell between those for either the "production" or the "ecology" scenarios (Zimmermann, 2012).

Source: Zimmermann, et al., 2011; Zimmermann, 2012.

and reallocating payments to better target specific objectives. The new policy sought to address conflicts with the World Trade Organisation's (WTO) "Green Box" criteria.[19]

Overall, the proposed policy for AP 2014-17 as set out in the Federal Council message in 2012 aimed to balance various interests. The major compromise consisted of maintaining the overall level of agricultural support (to appease supporters seeking to maintain the high levels of agricultural support) while re-distributing that support across the new categories of payments (to address demands of those supporting increased trade liberalisation as well as improving the environmental impact of payments).

The bill was then sent to Parliament, where it was debated by both chambers: the *Conseil des États* ("Council of States" or "Senate") and the *Conseil national* ("National Council" or "Chamber of Representatives"). The bill enjoyed broad support, but there were very divergent views on certain issues. The most contentious issue was the proposed removal of payments per head of cattle, which constituted an important fraction of overall payments, amounting to CHF 836 million in 2013, or 30% of total direct payments (Agrarbericht, 2014). Thus, the ultimate winners and losers of this element of reform were clearly identifiable. Animal husbandry payments were based on the number of cattle and were leading to intensification of livestock farm and thus increasing pressure on the environment. The payments were also not compliant with WTO Green Box rules. While the liberal, ecological and left-wing parties (FDP, Green Liberals and SP) supported the removal of these payments, the conservative-center and national-conservative parties (SVP and CVP), advocating for maintaining high levels of support to agriculture, were opposed, along with the Farmers' Union. Another critique of the reform was that it would increase the administrative burden on farmers, Cantons and the federal government, to implement a more complex system of payments[20] (Ritter, 2012).

The Parliament largely followed the proposal of the Federal Council, although the final total budgetary support agreed for the four-year period was CHF 160 million more than the CHF 13.83 billion set out in the message from the Federal Council (despite the fact that the number of farmers is decreasing) (NZZ, 2013). The additional CHF 160 million for the period was allocated to "basic improvements and social measures" (see Table 4.2). The budgeted amount of direct payments remained stable at around CHF 2.8 billion per year (the same level as 2012 and 2013) (OECD, 2015a).

Parliament approved the new legislation in March 2013, despite opposition of the SVP (NZZ, 2013). The Council of States voted unanimously (40-0) to approve the reform while the National Council voted to approve with 141 votes to 41 (NZZ, 2013). An alliance

Table 4.2. **Payments budget for Agricultural Policy 2014-17 (CHF millions)**

Measure	2014	2017	Total 2014-17
Basic improvements and social measures	**199**	**200**	**798**
Secondary social measures	3	3	12
Subsidies for structural improvements	99	99	396
Investment loans	47	47	188
Arable and cattle farming	38	38	153
Production and sales	**442**	**447**	**1 776**
Promotion and quality of sales	60	70	262
Dairy farming	296	296	1 184
Cattle farming	13	13	52
Arable farming	73	69	279
Direct payments	**2 814**	**2 814**	**11 256**
Subsidies for ensuring food supplies	1 094	1 094	4 376
Farmland subsidies	511	511	2 044
Subsidies for biodiversity	295	338	1 264
Subsidies for quality of landscape	20	90	210
Subsidies for production systems	361	403	1 526
Subsidies for efficient use of resources	52	73	256
Transition subsidies	482	306	1 579
Total	**3 455**	**3 461**	**13 830**

Source: Jarrett and Moeser (2013) updated from Lanz (2012).

between the FDP, SP and Green Liberals was able to bring together trade liberalisation and market-oriented concerns and ecological concerns to win support for the reform. It is questionable whether the AP 2014-17 would have been approved under the political composition of the Parliament in 2016. In April 2013, consultation on the comprehensive (300+ page) elaboration of the draft ordinance to specify the details of the implementation of the law took place, with farmers' organisations, including the Swiss Farmers' Union, closely engaged (NZZ, 2013).

Main aims of AP 2014-17 relating to biodiversity and the environment

Under the new AP 2014-17, direct payments to promote biodiversity were better aligned with policy goals promoting species and habitat diversity in agriculture (Box 4.4). In addition to continuing the specific category of biodiversity payments (which relates to improving the quality and networking of ECAs), biodiversity relevant aspects were also included in the new category of "landscape" payments. Payments for organic farming are paid out of the "production system" category. Environmental cross-compliance conditions are maintained in the new system of payments. Overall, the AP 2014-17 is seen as an important component of the Swiss biodiversity strategy[21] (FOAG, 2015).

The aims of the AP 2014-17 are summarised in Table 4.3. The new system of payments is complex, with each category including several programmes. These programmes are a combination of new programmes and "old" programmes that already existed under the previous agricultural policy. For example, the animal related payments under the previous system have been largely shifted to the category of food security payments (FOAG, 2012). In the case of biodiversity payments, this category reflects this mix of new and old programmes, as follows (OECD, 2015a):

- *Contribution to environmental quality level I* (pre-existing): regroups payments provided under ecological compensation in the former system

Box 4.4. **The contribution of the new direct payments system under the AP 2014-17 to biodiversity**

The new direct payments set out in AP 2014-17 promote biodiversity in a number of ways across the six new categories (in addition to transitional payments). These include:

Cultural landscape: Direct payments for the maintenance of cultural landscapes provide an incentive to prevent further overgrowing or forestation in order to conserve areas with high biodiversity quality in the alps and preserve their use for livestock in the summer.

Food supply: As part of the direct payments for sustaining food supply, there is an additional contribution for open agricultural cropland and permanent crops.

Biodiversity: Contributions for maintaining and promoting species and habitat diversity include payments for ecological compensation, biological quality and habitat linking. The quality of biodiversity is promoted through the differentiation of payments based on quality levels.

Landscape quality: Payments for landscape quality promote the conservation and evolution of diversity and quality of cultural landscapes.

Production system: Types of production which are in harmony with nature and are environmentally and animal friendly are promoted within the production systems contribution. This includes organic farming, extensive crop production (grains and rapeseed), animal-friendly housing and with opportunities for regular exercise as well as meat and milk production on grassland.

Resource efficiency: Payments are made to promote resource efficient techniques, such as pollution control procedures for slurry application, careful soil cultivation and precise procedures in pesticide application.

Source: FOAG, 2015.

Table 4.3. **Aims of the Swiss Agricultural Policy 2014-17**

Field	Aspect	Situation in 2007/09	Aims for 2017
Economy	Productivity	+2.1% p.a.	+2.1% p.a.
	Renewal of capital	30 years	30 years
Social	Incomes in the sector	-0.7% p.a.	Reduction in the drop in incomes to below 0.5% p.a.
Ensuring food supplies	Gross production	24 200 TJ	24 500 TJ
	Net production	21 500 TJ	22 100 TJ
	Farmed land in permanently settled areas	-1 900 ha p.a.	Reduction in loss of farmland to below 1 000 ha p.a.
Natural heritage, environment	N-efficiency	29%	33%
	P-efficiency	59%	68%
	NH_3 emissions	48 600 t N	41 000 t N
	Quantity of ESA	60 000 ha in lowland areas	65 000 ha in lowland areas
	Quality of ESA	36% interconnected 27% high-quality	50% interconnected 40% high quality
Farmland	Farmed land in mountain areas	-1 400 ha p.a.	Reduction in advance of woodland by 20%
Animal welfare	Participation in ROEL programmes	72%	80%

Note: "ESA" = ecological set-aside areas = Ecological Compensation Areas (ECAs).
Source: Lanz (2012).

- *Contribution to environmental quality level II* (pre-existing): corresponds to the payments provided under the Ecological Quality Directive in the former system
- *Contribution to environmental quality level III* (new): these payments are intended to finance projects listed as objectives of national importance, but have not yet been introduced.
- *Payments for ecological compensation areas* (pre-existing)
- *Payments for creating networks of highly valuable biodiversity areas* (new)

Impact of AP 2014-17 reforms so far

While it is too early to measure the impact of the AP 2014-17 on biodiversity, progress towards ecological goals is positive and participation in voluntary programmes funded by the biodiversity direct payments has exceeded expectations. Two of the three main environmental targets set for 2017 had already been reached before the new system of direct payments took effect. The target to reach 65 000 ha of ECAs in the plain region had already been achieved by 2013, with the total area climbing to over 71 000 ha in 2014. As illustrated in Figure 4.8, the target to have over 50% of ECAs participating in a regional networking project had already been reached in 2012 and climbed to over 65% in 2014. The share of ECAs meeting "Quality II" criteria has steadily increased and was nearly 34% in 2014, still short of the goal of 40% by 2017, although the target is well within reach. However, long term agri-environmental goals[22] have not yet been achieved.

Figure 4.8. **Increasing shares of Ecological Compensation Areas reaching Quality level II and included in Networking programmes, 2001-14**

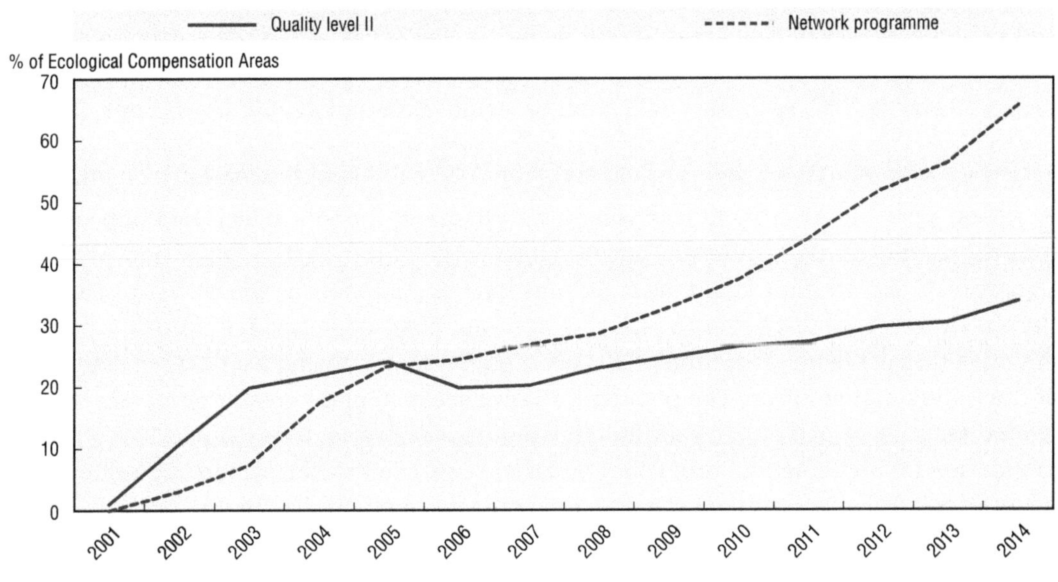

Source: Based on data from FOAG.

In 2014, biodiversity payments amounted to just over CHF 364 million, with 49% (CHF 179 million) allocated to ECAs of quality level I, 29% (CHF 105 million) for ECAs of quality level II and 22% (CHF 80 million) for including ECAs in a network. An additional CHF 40.4 million was paid for organic production and close to CHF 32 million for extensive production. Transition payments in 2014 amounted to close to CHF 308 million. Nearly 40% of direct payments in 2014 went to food security (CHF 1 096 million) (Agrarbericht, 2016). The distribution of 2014 direct payments across categories is shown in Figure 4.9.

Figure 4.9. **Distribution of direct payments by category, 2014**

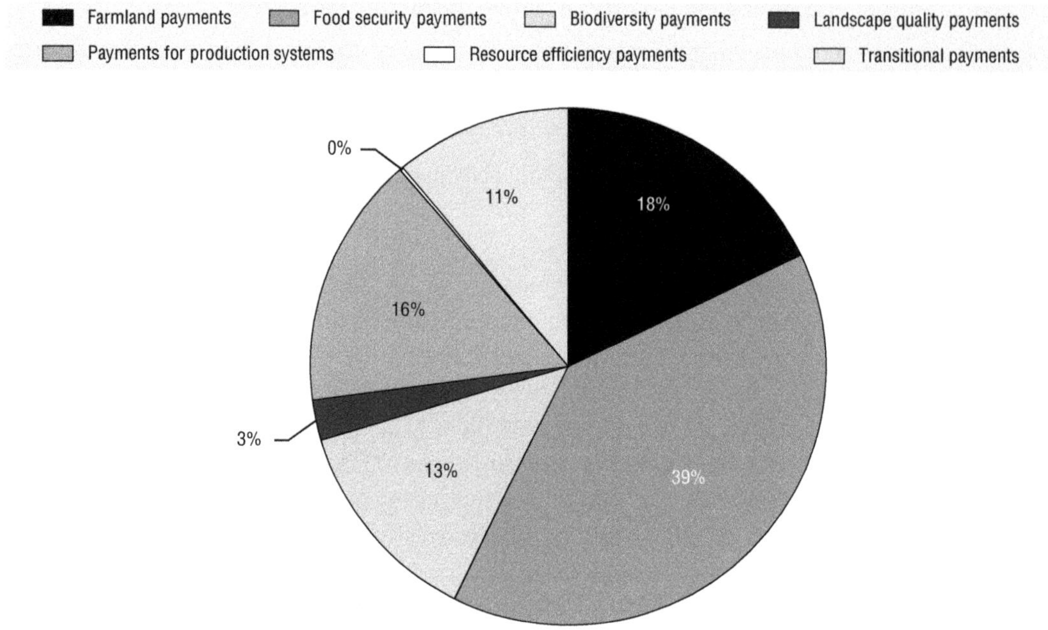

Source: Based on data from Agrarbericht, 2016.

To better understand the impact on biodiversity of the reform, a comprehensive monitoring programme (ALL-EMA)[23] is underway to assess the status and trends of species and habitats in agricultural areas. It will include a specific study of the current state and evolution of species in habitats in Ecological Compensation Areas. The first measurement cycle will end in 2019, with the publication of results expected in 2020 (Agroscope, 2016).

Recent developments: a push for food security and stabilising biodiversity payments

Soon after the AP 2014-17 was voted by Parliament, the SVP, which had opposed the reform, sought to call a referendum to overturn it (requiring the collection of 50 000 signatures). The attempt failed, as it did not have the support of the powerful Farmers' Union. However, in 2014, the Farmers' Union launched a successful call for a popular initiative (requiring the collection of 100 000 signatures) proposing a change to Article 104 of the Federal Constitution. The popular initiative seeks to place greater emphasis on goal of food security, as part of the multifunctional purpose of agriculture. Article 104 forms the foundation for Swiss Agricultural Policy and therefore, can have an important influence on how agricultural support under the direct payments system is allocated.

In response, the Federal Council adopted a message that, while recognising the importance of food security, rejected the initiative on the basis that food security is already very high in Switzerland and that the demands of the initiative are already largely addressed in the current Federal Constitution. Among the arguments put forth in the message, the Federal Council underlines that the government already support agricultural production with CHF 3.8 billion per year and that Swiss agriculture has reached, on average over the last three years, a record level in terms of production (FOAG, 2016). For the future, the Swiss government considers the following elements as crucial: 1) preserving the range and quality of farmland and reducing dependence on non-renewable resources; 2) ensuring the optimal exploitation of natural production; 3) improving the competitiveness of the Swiss food economy;

4) importing sufficient food and agricultural inputs ensuring access to international markets; and 5) conserving resources by reducing waste.

In Parliament, the Council of States is currently considering whether it will give a favourable recommendation or not to the initiative (the National Council has already given a favourable recommendation) before it is put to a vote by the Swiss public. In the meantime, the Council of States has requested that FOAG develop a counter-proposal to the original initiative proposal, which can then also be considered by the Swiss public at the time of the popular vote.

At the same time, considering the surprisingly high levels of participation in the voluntary programmes for biodiversity (specifically, for the Quality II of ECAs and networks), capping the total amount that can be paid under this category at CHF 400 million per year (of the total CHF 2.8 billion of direct payments per year)[24] is currently under discussion.[25] Parliament is discussing the AP 2018-21, which will likely maintain the total level of budgetary support to agriculture. Preparations for the Agricultural Policy from 2022 onwards are at a very early stage.

The environmental objectives for agriculture are in the process of being updated. The Federal Council has been requested[26] to submit a report to Parliament examining options to update objectives related ecosystem services and resource efficiency in agriculture to the before the end of 2016. The report will examine the extent to which the current environmental objectives for agriculture and the measures in place to achieve them could be improved (National Council, 2016).

4.4. Lessons learned

An alliance of market-oriented and ecological interests helped to spur reform

Arguably, the main impetus for the change in agricultural policy was support for market-oriented reforms to encourage free trade and bring the direct payments system more closely in alignment with WTO "Green Box" criteria. Concerns for biodiversity and ecosystems were important as well, but secondary, and helped to garner support for the reforms. Active lobbying by environmental NGOs as well as the leadership of the then Director of FOAG are also credited as reform drivers. Building a coalition among market-oriented interests promoting trade liberalisation and interests concerned with improving the environment were particularly crucial for advancing the reform.

Seizing a window of opportunity in a conducive political environment

The composition of the Parliament in 2013 provided a window of opportunity to adopt the reforms that had been in preparation over the preceding years. The Parliamentary elections in 2011 saw the Green Liberal Party successfully ride of wave of anti-nuclear sentiment in the aftermath of the disaster at Japan's Fukushima plant in March of that year (The Guardian, 2011). The current Parliament is more conservative, with greater representation of the SVP party, which had opposed the reform. It is questionable whether the AP 2014-17 would have been approved under the political composition of the current Parliament.

Devising politically and socially acceptable compromises in the reform package

The AP 2014-17 reflected important compromises that facilitated its approval by Parliament. This consisted of maintaining the overall level of budgetary support for agricultural (in fact, the overall level increased slightly) while re-distributing that support across the new categories of payments. Through this major compromise, the agricultural sector as a whole receives slightly increased budgetary payments over the 2014-17 period, while various groups of farmers either increase or decrease the level of direct payments they receive. For example, alpine farmers in particular benefitted from more payments for moving slopes, for extensive production and biodiversity payments under the new system, while farmers with intensive cattle operations in the lowland region of the country no longer receive payments per head of cattle.

It is important to note that interests across the agricultural sector are not homogenous, which was a facilitating factor for the reforms. Although the powerful Farmers' Union was against the reform, smaller lobby groups representing more specialised interests, such as organic farming or alpine farming, recognised that they were to be net beneficiaries of the changes and supported the reform. Environmental NGOs played a key role as part of their lobbying efforts to disseminate information about expected benefits of reforms to specialised agricultural groups, which encouraged their engagement.

Using transition payments to minimise negative impacts on farmers

The most contentious and hotly debated change in the reform package was the removal of payments per head of cattle. These payments constituted an important fraction of total payments for certain farmers and it was this element of the reform where the ultimate "losers" were clearly identifiable. To help offset expected income loses to farmers no longer receiving the payments per head of cattle, the reform package included transitional payments. In addition, the animal related payments under the previous system were largely shifted to the category of food security payments. At this stage, it is difficult to say how exactly these changes have affected farmers' incomes, as many variables affect production and farmers' incomes, or to what extent they may encourage structural change in the sector.

Influence of broad consultation and public participation

Switzerland has a unique political system, with elements of direct democracy such that political decision – making processes involve many stakeholders and extensive consultations. As a result, agreeing policy reforms and implementing them is a lengthy, but well-structured process (OECD, 2015a). In this case, broad stakeholder consultation helped to involve not only major lobbying groups including environmental NGOs, economics institutions, like economiesuisse, and the Farmers' Union, but also engaged smaller agricultural groups, including organic farmers associations and farmers located in alpine areas, who were well-positioned to benefit from the reform. Overall, this greater representativeness allowed for the inclusion of smaller groups, which could better express the heterogeneous interests of the agricultural sector. At the same time, there is a strong public consensus about the multi-function purpose of agriculture in the adoption of Article 104, which was adopted by popular vote. The outcome of the pending popular initiative on food security is yet to be seen.

While the AP 2014-17 represents an important step forward, Swiss agricultural subsidies remain relatively high compared to other OECD countries. The direct payments system still consists of a number of subsidies that have unclear, or possibly contradictory, impacts on environmental objectives. To continue to pursue biodiversity objectives and put Swiss agriculture on a more sustainable footing, the system will need to continue to evolve with better targeted direct payments.

Notes

1. The case study was prepared based on a literature review and interviews with the Swiss Federal Office of the Environment: Hans Gujer and Gabriela Blatter; the Swiss Federal Office of Agriculture: Jérôme Frei and Judith Ladner Callipari; Kathrin Bertschy, Member of Parliament; Marcel Liner, ProNatura; Werner Müller, Birdlife International; and Christophe Dietler, Agrarallianz. Other organisations were contacted with a request for an interview, including the Swiss Farmers' Union and economiesuisse, but did not respond.
2. Between 2009 and 2014, Utilised Agriculture Area (UAA) remained generally stable, with only a very slight decline.
3. Switzerland's UAA is composed of permanent grasslands (47%), alpine pasture (32%), arable land (18%) lands under permanent crops (2%) and other cultures (1%) (2006 data). The agricultural sector is dominated by animal production with cattle accounting for almost half of the Swiss agricultural proceeds. Crop production is mainly wheat, barley and grain maize (FOAG, 2015).
4. "Biotope" refers to the region of a habitat that is associated with a specific ecological community.
5. According to Environment Switzerland (2015), "The main causes [of biodiversity loss] are intensive agriculture, the channelling and use of water bodies for generating electricity, soil sealing, landscape fragmentation, and the spread of invasive alien species."
6. More specifically, due to intensive and no longer sustainable management practices, agricultural ecosystems, in particular, have suffered severe losses in terms of small structures such as hedges and dry-stone walls. This decline is also boosted by high levels of fertiliser and pesticide use, species-poor seeding practices and the use of mechanised management methods (FOEN, 2014).
7. For example, nitrogen surpluses decreased by 18% during the period from 1990-92 to 1997-99. Nitrogen surpluses subsequently increased by 4% from 2000-02 to 2006-08, largely explained by a rise in manure nitrogen inputs (OECD, 2015a).
8. Cross compliance links direct payments to compliance by farmers with basic standards related to the environment, food safety, animal and plant health and animal welfare. Standards also require maintain land in good agricultural and environmental condition (EC, 2016).
9. Ecosystem services are the benefits people obtain from ecosystems.
10. A positive externality is the benefit enjoyed by an unrelated third party as a result of an economic activity. This is in contrast to a negative externality, which is a cost borne by an unrelated third party as a result of an economic activity (e.g. pollution). Agricultural activity can generate both positive and negative externalities.
11. The OECD defines market price support as an indicator of the annual monetary value of gross transfers from consumers and taxpayers to agricultural producers arising from policy measures creating a gap between domestic producer prices and reference prices of a specific agricultural commodity measured at the farm-gate level.
12. However, agricultural support also still includes untargeted and distorting measures such as market price support, border protection, export subsidies and refunds, and input subsidies (Jarrett and Moeser, 2013).
13. From 1993-98, general direct payments consisted of non-commodity specific payments related to various criteria, including payments for general farm characteristics, payments for integrated production, and payments for farming in difficult conditions. These payments categories were adjusted in 1999, with the notable addition of a general payment for ruminants (OECD, 2015a).
14. The Federal Council is the seven-member executive council which constitutes the federal government of Switzerland and serves as the collective executive head of government and state of Switzerland. The current seven-member council are from the 4 leading political parties in Switzerland, namely the Swiss People's Party (SVP), Christian Democratic People's Party (CVP), Free Democratic Party of Switzerland (FDP) and the Social Democratic Party of Switzerland (SP).
15. Inconsistencies between policy instruments and objectives steering agricultural spending have created some distortions. For example, payments to maintain cattle production in geographically less favoured areas create incentives to increase stocking densities on grassland, which increases environmental pressures, conflicting with the environmental objectives supported by ecological direct payments (OECD, 2015a).
16. 09.3973 Motion CEAT-S: Revision of the direct payments system. A concrete concept, 16 October 2009.

17. Agrarallianz is an alliance bringing together 16 organisations working in the areas of consumer protection, environment and animal welfare, and economics.
18. This refers mainly to the general per hectare payment with no requirement other than cross-compliance, and which had served primarily as a measure of income support. The animal based payments for ruminants were also abandoned, causing a lot of criticism in a country whose agriculture is traditionally characterised by cattle and goats (Mann and Lanz, 2013).
19. WTO "Green Box" criteria include those payments that are allowed without limit. While the process of market-oriented reforms had generally been advancing in a positive direction, Swiss agricultural support remained almost three times the OECD average (WTO, 2013).
20. Markus Ritter, President of Swiss Farmers' Union noted, "The implementation – and this is my criticism – will cause a significant amount of administrative work, as many of the new instruments, which are to be introduced, will require appropriate planning and controls prior to their implementation, right down to the cantonal and operational level. We are also concerned that the strong focus of direct payments on the surface will exacerbate the market with respect to the leased land with higher rents" (Ritter, 2012).
21. In addition to the programmes under the direct payments system, Swiss agricultural policy supports other environmental programmes, such as the NAP-PGREL programme and the resource programme.
22. As set out in Walter et al. (2013) *Operationalisierung der Umweltziele Landwirtschaft* [Operationalisation of Environmental Goals for Agriculture].
23. The monitoring programme is called *Arten und Lebensräume Landwirtschaft – Espèces et milieux agricoles*, and referred to as ALL-EMA.
24. Although these categories are not directly comparable, it is notable that ecological direct payments under the previous system amounted to CHF 641 million and CHF 667 million in 2012 and 2013 respectively Agrarbericht, 2016).
25. For comparison, payments for biodiversity programmes in 2013 amounted to CHF 237 million (Agrarbericht, 2014).
26. Motion 13.4282 "Postulate Bertschy", adopted by the National Council.

References

Agrarbericht (2016), "Système des paiements directs" [Direct payments system], *www.agrarbericht.ch/fr/politique/paiements-directs/systeme-des-paiements-directs* (accessed 19 September 2016).

Agrarbericht (2014), *Rapport Agricole 2014* [Agricultural Report 2014], *www.agrarbericht.ch/fr/services/archive/rapport-agricole-2014* (accessed 4 October 2016).

Agroscope (2016), "Programme de monitoring, Espèces et milieux agricoles – ALL-EMA" [Monitoring programme, agricultural habitats and species.

Aviron, et al. (2008), "Ecological cross compliance promotes farmland biodiversity in Switzerland", *Front Ecol Environ* 2009; 7(5): 247-252, *http://dx.doi.org/10.1890/070197.*

Das Bundesamt für Umwelt (BAFU) and Bundesamt für Land-wirtschaft (BLW) (2008), *Umweltziele Landwirtschaft: Hergeleitet aus bestehenden rechtlichen Grundlagen,* [Environmental Objectives Agriculture: Derived from Existing Legal Bases], *www.bafu.admin.ch/publikationen/publikation/00097/index.html?lang=de* (accessed 30 August 2016).

Besser (2010), "The economic value of pollinating services in Switzerland", Contribution to The Economics of Ecosystems and Biodiversity (TEEB), *www.cbd.int/financial/values/switzerland-valuebees.pdf* (accessed 20 September 2016).

European Commission (EC) (2016), "Cross-compliance", *http://ec.europa.eu/agriculture/envir/cross-compliance/index_en.htm* (accessed 12 October 2016).

Federal Office for Agriculture (FOAG) (2016), "Initiative pour la sécurité alimentaire", [Initiative for food security], *www.blw.admin.ch/blw/fr/home/politik/ernaehrungssicherheit/intitiative-fuer-ernaehrungssicherheit.html* (accessed 22 September 2016).

Federal Office for Agriculture (FOAG) (2015), "Biodiversity for food and agriculture in Switzerland", Abridged version and main findings of *Switzerland's Country Report on the State of Biodiversity for Food and Agriculture*, Federal Office for Agriculture, Bern.

Federal Office for Agriculture (FOAG) (2012), "AP 14-17 Botschaft" [AP 14-17 Message], *www.blw.admin.ch/blw/de/home/politik/agrarpolitik/ap-14-17/ap-14-17---botschaft.html* (accessed 19 September 2016).

Federal Office for Agriculture (FOAG) (2009), "Weiterentwicklung DZ" [Further direct payments system],*www.blw.admin.ch/blw/de/home/politik/agrarpolitik/fruehere-reformetappen/weiterentwicklung-direktzahlungssystem.html* (accessed 19 September 2016).

Federal Office for Agriculture (FOAG) (2004), *Swiss Agricultural Policy: Objectives, Tools, Prospects*, *www.cbd.int/financial/pes/swiss-pesagriculturalpolicy.pdf* (accessed 24 May 2016).

Federal Office for Agriculture (FOAG) (n.d.), *Swiss Agriculture on the Move: the New Agricultural Act Ten Years On*, FOAG, Berne.

Federal Office for the Environment (FOEN) (2016), "The Swiss case: Greening through different approaches outside the CAP in Europe", presentation, 20 April 2016.

Federal Office for the Environment (FOEN) (2014), *5th National Report to the Convention on Biological Diversity*.

Federal Statistical Office (FSO) (2015), *Swiss Agriculture: Pocket Statistics 2015*, FSO, Neuchâtel.

Finger and Lehmann (2012), "Adoption of agri-environmental programmes in Swiss crop production", *EuroChoices*, 11(1), The Agricultural Economics Society and the European Association of Agricultural Economists.

Grabs, J (2013), *Differences between EU-CAP proposals and the new supporting scheme of the Swiss agriculture from 2014, https://foodpolicyforthought.files.wordpress.com/2013/05/differences-eu-and-switzerland.pdf.*

Jarrett, P. and C. Moeser (2013), "The Agri-food situation and policies in Switzerland", *OECD Economics Department Working Papers*, No. 1086, OECD Publishing, Paris, *http://dx.doi.org/10.1787/5k40d6ccd1jg-en.*

Lanz, S. (2012), "Article on economics: Main aspects of the Agricultural Policy for 2014-2017", Federal Office for Agriculture, Berne.

Lanz S. et al. (2010), *Weiterentwicklung des Direktzahlungssystems, Agrarforschung Schweiz*, [Further Development of the Direct Payments System, Agricultural Research in Switzerland] 1(1), 10-17, 2010

Lehman, B. and S. Lanz (2012), "Les grandes lignes de la politique agricole 2014-2017", [The main directions of agricultural policy 2014-2017], *La Vie économique, Revue de politique économique*, 4-2012, pp. 4-8.

Loser, E. (2010) "The Swiss political approach to ensure ecological compensation in the agricultural landscape", Swiss Federal Office for Agriculture, presentation at the High Nature Value Farmland in Europe Conference in Vilm, 14-18 June 2010.

National Council (2016), "Bases naturelles de la vie et efficacité des ressources dans la production agricole. Actualisation des objectifs", [Ecosystem services and resource efficiency in agriculture : updating objectives], *Postulat* 13.4284, *www.parlament.ch/fr/ratsbetrieb/suche-curia-vista/geschaeft?AffairId=20134284* (accessed 21 September 2016).

Neue Zürcher Zeitung (NZZ) (2013), "Die reform der agrarpolitik ist unter dach" [The reform of agricultural policy is underway], 23 March 2013, *www.nzz.ch/schweiz/die-reform-der-agrarpolitik-ist-unter-dach-1.18052107* (accessed 25 May 2016).

OECD (2015a), *OECD Review of Agricultural Policies: Switzerland 2015*, OECD Publishing, Paris, *http://dx.doi.org/10.1787/9789264168039-en.*

OECD (2015b), *OECD Economic Surveys: Switzerland 2015*, OECD Publishing, Paris, *http://dx.doi.org/10.1787/eco_surveys-che-2015-en.*

OECD (2013), *OECD Compendium of Agri-environmental Indicators*, OECD Publishing, Paris, *http://dx.doi.org/10.1787/9789264186217-en.*

Ritter, M. (2012), *Current Concerns*, 10 December, 2012. No. 51. ISSN 1664-7963, *www.voltairenet.org/IMG/pdf/CC_1012_2012_51.pdf* (accessed 30 August 2016).

Swissinfo.ch (2016), "Farmers receive more for biodiversity and summer grazing", *www.swissinfo.ch/eng/agriculture-reforms_farmers-receive-more-for-biodiversity-and-summer-grazing/42060944* (accessed 24 May 2016).

The Guardian (2011), "Swiss election sees nationalist party lose share of votes", 23 October 2011, *www.theguardian.com/world/2011/oct/23/swiss-election-nationalist-party-result* (accessed 21 September 2016).

Tschumi, M. et al. (2016), "Perennial, species-rich wildflower strips enhance pest control and crop yield", *Agriculture, Ecosystems and Environment*, 220, pp. 97-103, *http://dx.doi.org/10.1016/j.agee.2016.01.001*.

Tschumi, M. et al. (2015), "High effectiveness of tailored flower strips in reducing pests and crop plant damage" *Proceedings of the Royal Society B*, 282:20151369, *http://dx.doi.org/10.1098/rspb.2015.1369*.

Walter, T. et al. (2013), "Operationalisierung der umweltziele landwirtschaft" [Operationalisation of the environmental objectives for agriculture", Agroscope Reckenholz-Tänikon (ART).

World Trade Organization (WTO) (2013), *Trade Policy Review, Review by the Secretariat: Switzerland and Liechtenstein*, WT/TPR/S/280, 19 March.

Zandonella, R. et al. (2014), *Le Coût Économique de l'Utilisation de Pesticides en Suisse – Compte Pilote*, [The Economic Cost of the Use of Pesticides in Switzerland – Pilot Study], INFRAS.

Zimmermann, A (2011), "Les conséquences d'une réforme du système des paiements directs; Simulations à l'aide de modèles SILAS et SWISSland" [The consequences of the reform of the system of direct payment : simulations with the aid of the SILAS and SWISSland models], *Rapport ART 744*, DFE, Agroscope Reckenholz-Tänikon, March.

Zimmermann, A. et al. (2012), *Auswirkungen der Agrarpolitik 2014-2017, Aktualisierung der wichtigsten Ergebnisse des ART-Berichts Nr. 744*, [Consequences of the Agricultural Policy for 2014-2017, Update of the Principle Results Set out in ART Report no. 744], Agroscope Reckenholz Tänikon. *www.agrarallianz.ch/uploads/media/ART_Auswirkungen_Beitragsszenarien_AP_14-17.pdf* (accessed 30 August 2016).

The Political Economy of Biodiversity Policy Reform

Chapter 5

EU payments to Mauritania and Guinea-Bissau for MPA conservation under the Fisheries Partnership Agreements

This chapter examines efforts to establish sustainable financing for marine protected areas in the biodiversity-rich West African countries of Mauritania and Guinea-Bissau. The case study focusses on how both countries secured financial resources from Fisheries Partnership Agreements with the European Union to capitalise conservation trust funds that are intended to provide long-term and sustainable financing for marine protected areas. This case study draws lessons from the political economy aspects of establishing and capitalising these trust funds. It emphasises the importance of building a shared understanding of the benefits of marine ecosystems to an economically important industry. It also highlights the role of environmental NGOs to secure agreement among key actors and how advances to secure sustainable financing for marine conservation can be threatened by changing political priorities.

Introduction

The coast of West Africa has been identified as a marine eco-region of global importance. The region's fisheries are an important contributor to GDP, providing livelihoods for fishers and processors, as well as a source of hard currency (from exports of fishery products). Fisheries also boost government revenues through fisheries agreements and taxes. The pressure on West African fish stocks increased considerably over the past decades, mainly due to over-fishing. In Mauritania and Guinea-Bissau, conservation trust funds were created to provide sustainable financing to marine protected areas (MPAs) with the objective of channelling funds, including from the European Union (EU) through Fisheries Partnership Agreements. This case study demonstrates how concerted lobbying efforts by environmental NGOs established a shared understanding of the benefits that marine conservation could bring to the fisheries sector. It also highlights how wavering political support as a result of changing leadership can threaten the long-term stability of financing for conservation and the importance of a secure legal basis for agreements to avoid back-sliding.

5.1. Conserving marine biodiversity as the basis for sustainable fisheries in West Africa

The coast of West Africa, from Mauritania in the North to Sierra Leone 3 200 km in the South, has been identified as a Marine Ecoregion[1] of global importance, essential in maintaining regionally and globally threatened biodiversity (WWF Wamer and Wetlands International, 2007). Cape Verde for example, harbours one of the most important coral reefs in the world with numerous unique and rare species, making it a one of ten global hot-spots for coral communities (Roberts et al., 2002). Guinea-Bissau hosts the largest mangrove area in West Africa and the most important green turtle nesting site in West and Central Africa, on the Island of Poilão (Catry et al., 2009; 2002). Cap Blanc, Mauritania has one of the largest remaining sub-populations of the endangered Mediterranean monk seal. More than two million shorebirds spend the northern winter in the Banc d'Arguin National Park (PNBA) in Mauritania, which protects one of several coastal areas critical for migratory birds all along the West African coast (Engelmoer et al., 1984; Wolff et al., 1993).

The up-welling of cold water and nutrients in the West African Marine Ecoregion supports a fishing zone of global importance, that makes a significant contribution to the local economies of coastal states in the ecoregion (Diop and Scheren, 2016). In addition to supplying food, fishing activities contribute to gross domestic product (GDP), provide livelihoods for fishers and processors, provide a source of hard currency (from exports of fishery products), and boost government revenues through fisheries agreements and taxes (de Graaf and Garibaldi, 2014). Fish contributes to at least 20% of the total animal protein intake in the coastal countries of West Africa (FAO, 2009). Fishing activities are a major contributor to GDP in the West African Marine Ecoregion, ranging from 5% of GDP in Mauritania (COFREPECHE, NFDS, POSEIDON and MRAG, 2014) to 2.51% in The Gambia, compared to an African average of 1.26% according to FAO (de Graaf and Garibaldi, 2014). The fishing industry directly employs around 129 000 people in Senegal, 40 000 in The Gambia, and 64 000 in Guinea (de Graaf, G. and Garibaldi, 2014).

Over-fishing is currently the main threat to marine and coastal ecosystems in West Africa (WWF Wamer and Wetlands International, 2007), although coastal development, oil industry, pollution, and climate change, are also key concerns. More specifically, the pressure on West African fish stocks increased six-fold between the 1960s and the1990s, due to fishing by European, Russian and Asian fleets (Hogan, 2003), but also as a result of the substantial expansion of artisanal fisheries (Matthew, 2003). The impact of overfishing is several orders of magnitude greater than that of the unsustainable fishing practices of small-scale artisanal fisheries (with the use of destructive fishing gear) (Diop and Scheren, 2016; Failler, 2006).

NGOs have played an important role in efforts towards the implementation of sustainable fishing in the West African Ecoregion, at least for the European fleets (Brown, 2005; Failler, 2006; IEEP, 2002). In 2004, the European Council paved the way for a new generation of agreements, the Fisheries Partnership Agreements (FPAs),[2] to allow EU vessels to fish for surplus stocks in foreign exclusive economic zones (EEZs) (EC, 2015). These agreements focus on resource conservation, environmental sustainability,[3] and contribute to the social and economic development of the partner countries. In exchange, the EU provides a financial contribution to the partner countries, which includes two components: 1) a financial contribution for access rights to the fisheries resources within the EEZ (which can be used at the discretion of the partner country) and 2) "sectoral" financial support, which aims to promote sustainable fisheries development in the partner countries and is spent according to an agreed programming (depending on the needs identified by the partner country) (EC, 2015). In addition, EU-vessel owners also pay for licenses for fish-catches.

In the West Africa Marine Ecoregion, the FPA initiated in 2006 with Mauritania was the EU's single largest agreement, both in financial terms (EUR 86 million a year directly from the EU), and in terms of fisheries opportunities (approximately 200 licences were available for European vessels to fish in Mauritanian waters) (EC, 2007). The agreement has recently been renewed, committing EUR 59 million per year to the partnership, with EUR 4 million supporting the fishing communities, including environmental sustainability, job creation and tackling illegal and unregulated fishing. Others countries of the Ecoregion with a FPA with the EU include Cape Verde, Guinea-Bissau, and Senegal.

Compared to the purely commercial agreements,[4] the FPAs seek to reinforce the development dimension of the EU agreements (EC, 2007). The financial contributions made by the EU are a very significant source of revenue for fisheries administrations and, in some cases, the economy of partner countries as a whole (The evaluation partnership, Poseidon, MRAG, 2010). In 2009, the total EU contributions were 15 times the national budget for fisheries in Mauritania and accounted for more than 16% of the country's total public revenues; the EU contribution is comparable in Guinea-Bissau (15.6% of total public revenues) (Oceana, 2011).

While the new generation of fisheries agreements are an improvement compared to simple access agreements, their practical implementation could be improved (European Court of Auditors, 2015; Ould Ahmed Salem, 2012). A 2015 report by the European Court of Auditors concluded that the FPAs are generally well managed by the European Commission, but that there are still areas for improvement in terms of the negotiation process and the implementation of protocols. In principle, the FPAs should only allow EU vessels to fish the surplus resources of partner countries. However, this concept of surplus is very difficult to apply in practice due to lack of reliable information on fish stocks and fishing effort of the various fleets. Further, the report found that the implementation of access conditions was not sufficiently robust and the Commission's role in monitoring implementation of the protocols was limited (European Court of Auditors, 2015). Earlier reviews of FPAs have raised similar concerns about the effectiveness of the agreements in improving sustainable fisheries management.

Even with such mixed results, FPAs play an important role in the wider effort to improve the sustainability of fisheries. The recognition of the EU's responsibility in promoting sustainable fishing activities and the conservation of marine resources, especially in developing countries,[5] has been highlighted by the European Economic and Social Committee. Furthermore, on 10 December 2015 the European Commission adopted a proposal to revise the Regulation 1006/2008 on fishing authorisations[6] in view of regulatory developments on illegal, unreported and unregulated fishing (European Parliament, 2015), to promote transparent and sustainable fisheries.

In addition to limiting overfishing, establishing MPAs can also help to conserve marine biodiversity. Countries in the West African region have a long experience of MPA establishment and management: the National Parks of *Banc d'Arguin* (Mauritania), *Langue de Barbarie* and *Sine Saloum* Delta (Senegal), for example, were created as early as 1976. The identification of ecological corridors between MPAs, and the pooling of countries' conservation efforts and needs resulted in the establishment of a regional network of MPAs in West Africa in 2007, which currently comprises 23 MPAs (WWF, 2005; Kimball, 2003).

Management of MPAs typically involves zoning different areas with different types or levels of permitted use, including fishing. For instance, many MPAs in Guinea-Bissau allow fishing by people living in and around them, with restrictions on the technology or gear they may use. Many MPAs in the Ecoregion also include areas that are strictly closed to fishing. Thus, the distinction between fishing regulations to promote sustainable use, and regulations creating MPAs can be blurry as they sometimes overlap. Nevertheless, regulating fishing practices and establishing MPAs forms the basis for a policy mix of "sea-sharing" and "sea-sparing"[7] that can benefit both biodiversity and fishing. Indeed, the effectiveness of MPAs in ensuring more sustainable fisheries has been documented in many cases (Garcia et al., 2013; Guénette et al., 2014; OECD, forthcoming).

5.2. Opportunities for innovative financing of marine protected areas

An important challenge for effective MPA management in West Africa is long term financing. In a context where national capacities for government funding of MPA management are low, project-based support by international donors has played an important role. In general, donor funding for MPAs is part of a wider portfolio of finance, and tends to support establishment costs, training, and other forms of capacity building, as well as putting frameworks in place for them to become financially self-sufficient (OECD, forthcoming). Such support, however, is mostly short-term and vulnerable to changes in donor priorities (Carr-Dirick and Klug, 2002).

Conservation trust funds (CTFs) have been proposed as an innovative solution to this challenge. CTFs have been defined as "private, legally independent grant-making institutions that provide sustainable financing for biodiversity conservation and often finance part of the long-term management costs of a country's protected area system" (CFA, 2008). Their main advantages and challenges and some distinctions among stakeholders are summarised in Table 5.1.

Table 5.1. **Advantages and challenges related to conservation trust funds**

	All stakeholders	
Advantages	Funds can provide a vehicle for collaboration among the government, NGOs, and the private sector. Capacity to involve a wide range of stakeholders with participatory structures. Capacity to attract a diverse range of national and international funding sources. Funds are a stable, long-term source of funding, allow long-term planning and strategy implementation.	
	Local stakeholders (e.g. governments)	**External stakeholders (e.g. donors)**
Advantages for specific stakeholders	Capacity to avoid much of the bureaucracy of large donor or financial agencies.	Funds are politically independent, and therefore ensure continuity from one government to another. Capacity to absorb major amounts of funding and disburse it over time.
	All stakeholders	
Challenges	Funds can result in decreased government or donor spending and commitment in these areas. Funds require highly technical, expensive and sophisticated management skills for the fund administration. Funds can face enormous pressure to disburse funds, particularly after lengthy start-up phases. Funds can finance activities disconnected with national environment strategies and priorities.	
	Local stakeholders	**External stakeholders**
Challenges for specific stakeholders	Funds tie up substantial amounts of scarce resources, and often generate modest amounts of income. Funds give direction and control of potentially large sums of resources to independent organisations (although governments and donors may be represented on their boards).	Funds can be overwhelmed with demands for resources from a variety of sources (often well beyond the environmental groups originally involved).

Source: Adapted from GEF Secretariat, 1998.

In Mauritania and Guinea-Bissau, CTFs were created to provide sustainable financing to MPAs with the objective of channelling funds from a range of donors, including funds received from the EU via FPAs. This can be considered akin to an international payments for ecosystem services (PES) scheme in both countries,[8] given the definition by Wunder (2015).

5.3. The creation of conservation trust funds and their capitalisation

BACoMaB and EU-Mauritania Fisheries Partnership Agreements

The impetus for establishing a trust fund for marine conservation in Mauritania emerged in the early 2000, in a context of declining donor support (Beddiyouh, 2016). Conservation organisations working in Mauritania began to explore ways of achieving more sustainable financing for the PNBA. A feasibility study for the creation of a trust fund for the PNBA was undertaken, commissioned by the PNBA and partners (WWF, GTZ, FIBA). It proposed, among other measures, that the government of Mauritania capitalise the trust fund in part with funds received under the FPA with the EU (Carr-Dirick and Klug, 2002). This would be considered as a financial contribution by the governments, thereby following recommendations by the Global Environment Facility (GEF) for the creation of CTFs (GEF Secretariat, 1998).

Lobbying, co-ordination of stakeholder interests and actions then followed. This was driven, in particular, by the *Fondation Internationale du Banc d'Arguin* (FIBA[9]), a long-term partner of PNBA with a strong influence on conservation in Mauritania (Goyet, 2016; Renaud, 2016). Persistent and determined lobbying of different institutions of the EU (DG

Fisheries, DG Research, DG Development, DG Environment) between 2003 and 2005 led to their endorsement of the idea of financing MPAs for their role in the conservation and sustainable use of fisheries resources (Goyet, 2016). This generated support by the highest authorities in the EU (Office of the President of the European Commission) for PNBA to be a key element of FPAs with Mauritania (Goyet, 2016).

Lobbying of the EU resulted in an annual allocation within the FPA to finance the PNBA.[10] The first protocol (2006-08) of the 2006-12 FPA came with financial compensation for access by EU vessels to Mauritania's waters (EUR 75 million per annum)[11] and financial support for the implementation of the national fisheries policy to enhance responsible fishing and the sustainable exploitation of fisheries resources (EUR 11 million per annum). Of this EUR 11 million of sectoral support, the protocol also clearly stated EUR 1 million per annum should be allocated to funding the PNBA (Official Journal of the European Union, 2006, Article 2, paragraphs 1, 5). Financial contributions by the EU to PNBA therefore, i) echoed the principle of resource conservation on which the European fisheries policy is based, ii) were based on the results of research within the PNBA that identified the Banc d'Arguin as a key contributor to the fish resources (Guénette et al., 2014), and iii) were linked to the sectoral financial support included in the FPA with Mauritania. Support to PNBA represented 1.62% of the FPA (EUR 86 million in total), which was considered acceptable by the Government of Mauritania (Appriou, 2016).

The creation of the BACoMaB Trust Fund in 2009, under English Law,[12] was also a key factor in securing support for the PNBA (Goyet, 2016). Donors considering contributions to the trust fund, however, also raised the issue of additionality. They were concerned that BACoMaB would substitute state support for PNBA (Beddiyouh, 2016).

To ensure support by the Mauritanian government, conservation organisations also lobbied the highest government authorities, including the Ministry of Environment and PNBA itself (Goyet, 2016). The PNBA Director also lobbied the EU to secure funds for the BACoMaB (Appriou, 2016). The commitment of the Mauritanian government was reflected in the National Finance Act of 2007, where EUR 1 million per annum is earmarked for PNBA, thereby guaranteeing that the transfer would take place. The 2006-12 FPA did not mention direct support for the trust fund, which was only created in 2009. Nevertheless, the original idea was to use part of the revenues from the EU FPAs as a government contribution to the BACoMaB Trust Fund that was then being put in place (Goyet, 2016).

Persistent lobbying of the executive of PNBA by conservation organisations also led to the director of PNBA and the Minister of Environment to agree, in 2007, to allocate 50% of the funds received by PNBA under the FPAs (EUR 500 000 per year) to the endowment of the future trust fund (Goyet, 2016). The rationale for PNBA was that the funds it was going to receive under the FPAs largely exceeded its absorption capacity. In this context, transferring part of the funding to an endowment seemed appropriate (Beddiyouh, 2016). The financing scheme implemented in Mauritania is illustrated in Figure 5.1.

The trust fund is not funded directly. Under the FPA, the EU provides sectoral support funds that are paid into Mauritania's national budget. The Mauritanian government then channels part of the sectoral financial support (EUR 1 million per annum in the 2006-08 and 2008-12 protocols) to the PNBA. Until 2013, the PNBA then contributed to the endowment of the BACoMaB trust fund.[13] Therefore, another potential funding channel, allowing direct contribution from Mauritanian government to the BACoMaB trust fund (the black arrow in Figure 5.1), is under discussion by parties in the context of negotiations for future

Figure 5.1. **Funding marine protected areas in Mauritania from Fisheries Partnership Agreements through a conservation trust fund**

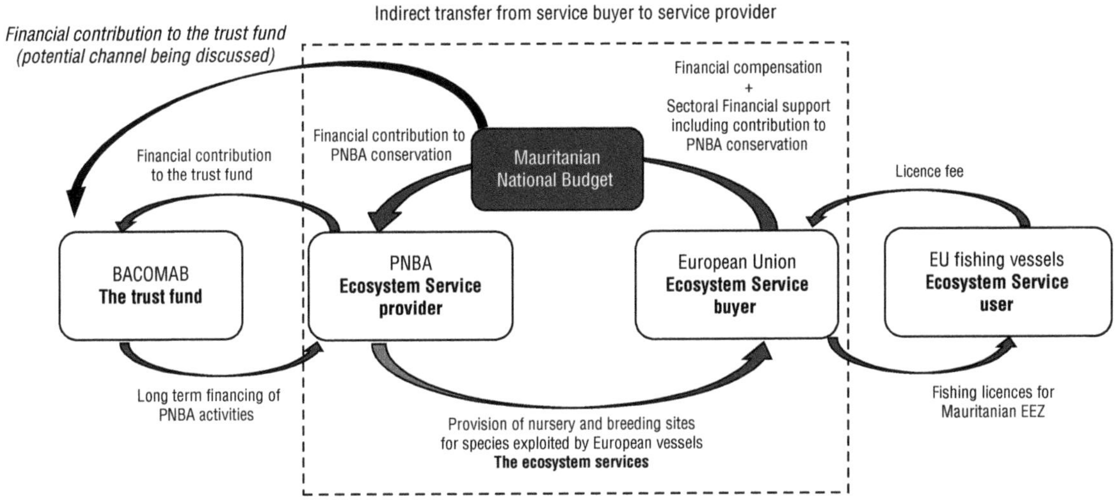

Source: Adapted from Binet et al., 2013.

agreements (see discussion below). The government's commitment to contribute to the BACoMaB trust fund has been a key factor in attracting additional contributions from others partners, such as the French Development Agency *(Agence Française de Développement)* (Chiron, 2016), KfW and the MAVA foundation.

As of April 2015, commitments to endow BACoMaB had reached EUR 22.3 million, of which EUR 21.3 million has been disbursed. The Mauritanian government has contributed EUR 2.8 million from the 2006-08 and 2008-12 protocols of the FPA (of which EUR 1.8 million has been disbursed). AFD has disbursed EUR 3.5 million (including EUR 1 million from the French Global Environment Fund, *Fonds Français pour l'Environnement Mondial*). KfW and MAVA have disbursed EUR 10 and 6 million respectively. For a trust fund established as recently as 2009, this level of capitalisation is very satisfactory according to some observers. It has, however, been achieved progressively, which means that the trust fund has yet to be a major source of support for conservation activities in Mauritania (Lefghih, 2016). Between 2014 and 2016, the trust fund disbursed grants for EUR 650 000 euros, for coastal and maritime surveillance, conservation, and research activities (BACoMaB, 2015). The evolution of the implementation of BACoMaB is illustrated in Figure 5.2.

Fundação BioGuinea trust fund and EU-Guinea-Bissau Fisheries Partnership Agreements

The protected areas system of Guinea-Bissau has gone through important changes since 2000 during a period of normalisation following the 1998-99 civil war and the subsequent return of international donors. Prior to 2000, parks were poorly managed ("paper parks"), with limited support by donors. In the early 2000s, the World Bank and the United Nations Development Programme convened a dialogue in Guinea-Bissau on the necessary institutional arrangements for protected areas resulting in a recommendation to create an Institute of Biodiversity and Protected Areas (IBAP) to bring all protected areas under one roof for more co-ordinated management. This received strong support from donors and led to the funding of several projects. It was in this context that a discussion on establishing a foundation with an endowment fund was initiated in Guinea-Bissau

Figure 5.2. **The establishment of the BACoMaB Trust Fund and its funding through the Fisheries Partnership Agreement**

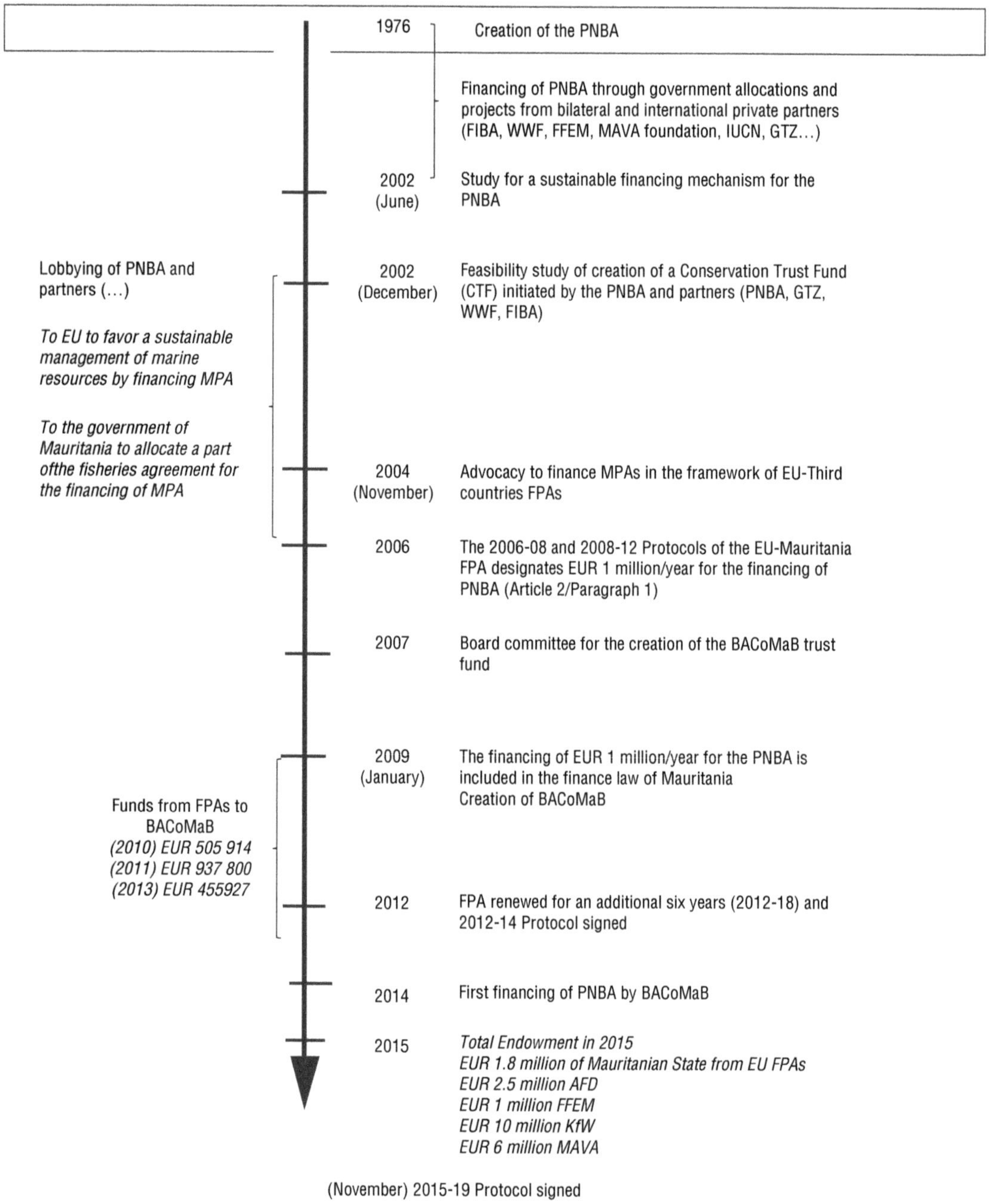

Source: Interviews with: Appriou, 2016; Beddiyouh, 2016; Chiron, 2016; Goyet, 2016; Lefghih, 2016; Renaud, 2016.

(Yudelman, 2016). A first version of the foundation was created, in the country, with a grant from WWF, however, inspired by the Mauritanian and other country experiences, it was decided to shift the foundation offshore. A second and final version of the trust fund was established under English law in 2011.

As a result of a growing understanding of the relationship between management of coastal and marine protected areas (IBAP's domain) and sustainable management of fisheries (the Ministry of Fisheries' domain) a dialogue was launched and an agreement reached, in principle, on the relevance of contributing fisheries funds to support of the management of these important coastal and marine protected areas and the fish breeding and nursery grounds they sustain. The link was thus made between the conservation of the coastal environment and the fisheries of Guinea-Bissau and beyond. This shared understanding at the technical level, ensured this commitment was sustained despite the frequent turn over in governments engendered by Guinea-Bissau's political instability.

The government of Guinea-Bissau agreed to contribute to the future endowment of the trust fund (i.e. before the foundation was created in 2011) (Goyet, 2016; Renaud, 2016). The government was committed to securing USD 1 million, and funds from sectoral support included in FPA were a potential source for this commitment (Yudelman, 2016). The EU was a strong supporter of the process as they had been involved from the beginning. It was a local discussion with the EU delegation, with DG MARE following the process from a distance (Yudelman, 2016). At the end of 2014, during the negotiations for programming FPA's sectoral support, the government of Guinea-Bissau negotiated that the EU support half of USD 1 million commitment as a contribution to the Fundação BioGuinea Trust Fund (FBG) (Bastos, 2016).

The FBG and its trust fund was legally established and registered in 2011 under English Law and has a charitable organisation status in UK with a host agreement allowing it to operate in Guinea-Bissau. A core objective of its mission is to generate sustainable finance for the benefit of the national system of protected areas and biodiversity in Guinea-Bissau. The trust fund is currently in the process of securing its initial seed capital. Commitments in the order of EUR 5 million have been received, which include EUR 1 million from the government, of which USD 500 000 is to be drawn from the sectoral support included in the 2014-17 Protocol of the FPA with the EU (as specified in the approved joint programming for 2015), and the rest from others sources (Bastos, 2016) . The first tranche of EUR 500 000 was transferred by the government to the FBG in January 2016.

The experience of BACoMaB was a key factor in the creation of the FBG trust fund in Guinea-Bissau. The same international partners were involved in conservation in both countries. The enthusiasm and willingness of particular advocates for the scheme, including people in government was also an important factor of success.

The creation of a CTF in Guinea-Bissau and its funding through the FPA with the EU were successful, in part, thanks to a favorable institutional context for conservation. This context had been encouraged by various laws enacted between 1997 and 2011, which led to the establishment of a network of protected areas including several MPAs, and the creation, in 2005, of IBAP. Both IBAP and FBG are autonomous, financially and otherwise, and the directors are competitively selected (rather than being nominated). This has enabled continuity in leadership, which is harder to achieve in government agencies and Ministries. Another factor of success was that the arrangement built on prior initiatives and the long term engagement of NGOs such as IUCN and FIBA. Gaining support takes time, but the absence of pre-existing institutions (such as government-led park agencies or funding bodies) that could have blocked change also facilitated the process. The creation of the current set of institutions and the arrangement described here took place as many of the country's institutions were being rebuilt following the civil war.

5.4. Challenges to effective implementation of the conservation trust funds

Several challenges have been encountered in the long term effective implementation of the CTFs in both Mauritania and Guinea-Bissau. First, political acceptance of the arrangement has been limited by insufficient awareness of the importance of the conservation efforts and their need for sustainable financing. In Mauritania, the commitment of the government to establish a PES via the FPA seems to have been insufficient and lacked stability. This is evidenced in the decrease of its support for the PNBA over subsequent protocols, which is largely attributable to the changes in the perspectives of Mauritanian authorities over time (Appriou, 2016). For example, the first two Protocols (2006-08 and 2008-12) of the 2006-12 FPA clearly stated the share of the sectoral support (EUR 1 million of the 11 million, annually) that should be allocated to the PNBA. The following Protocols (2012-14 and 2015-19) significantly reduced sectoral support (EUR 3 million and EUR 4.125 million, respectively).

Negotiations for the two most recent Protocols (2012-14 and 2015-19) to earmark funding for MPAs through CTFs were difficult. Although the EU remains committed to the idea, new staff at the Mauritanian Ministry of Environment and the PNBA, who had not been involved in the establishment of the original agreement, challenged the rationale for contributing to the endowment, in a context where government priorities had shifted (Goyet, 2016). Moreover, at the institutional level, the current PNBA director is not systematically willing to transfer funds to the BACoMaB (Appriou, 2016; Beddiyouh, 2016).

Difficulties and delays in the actual disbursement of funds committed by the government were another political barrier for the financing scheme to achieve effective outcomes. The original commitment stipulated that the BACoMaB should have received half of EUR 6 million, over the period of the 2006-12 Protocols. However, as of 2014, only EUR 2 million had been paid into the endowment (Goyet, 2016). Difficulties in disbursements are due, in part, to the fact that until 2012, single payments were made to the Ministry of Finance under sectorial support and the broader financial compensation for access to the fisheries resources (Appriou, 2016). Under the EU's Common Fisheries Policy (CFP), sectoral support is decoupled from the business side of the agreements.[14] This is more effective in terms of conditionality, including transferring of funds to PNBA, as payments for sectoral support may be canceled if conditions are not met (Appriou, 2016).

The FPA contributed to increase significantly Mauritania's budget for the conservation of marine and coastal protected areas. Distributing this financial support among different, competing, stakeholders is a challenge, which can stifle reform in favour of marine biodiversity in Mauritania. In Mauritania, PNBA and BACoMAB compete for FPA funds, in spite of their supposedly shared interest for conserving the Banc d'Arguin. The current executives of the PNBA wish to benefit from the totality of the FPA funds and regularly criticise the legal basis for channeling funds to BACoMAB, stating that the CTF itself is not mentioned in the Protocols, or in the Mauritanian budget law of 2007. The government's contribution is based on a legally questionable agreement between the Director of PNBA in 2013 (which has since been replaced by a new Director) and the BACoMaB (Beddiyouh, 2016). This has offered the legal basis for the current Director of PNBA to challenge the use of PNBA funds for the endowment of BACoMaB (Beddiyouh, 2016).

The use of the trust funds has also been challenged because of a perceived lack of effectiveness. Specifically, the delay in getting BACoMaB capitalised has meant that 4 years separate the first allocation of government funds (2010) and the first grants made to park authorities (2014). In addition, the funds are not fully in the hands of government authorities,[15] which generates frustration (Appriou, 2016; Lefghih, 2016). Moreover, the grants made by BACoMaB (EUR 650 000) represent a small proportion of the amount of capital tied up in the endowment (EUR 22.3 million) and the decision to allocate funds to an endowment has been further challenged in the context of low interest rates. As a result, the PNBA has suspended request for disbursement to BACoMaB since 2013 (Lefghih, 2016).

Donors, however, remain supportive to a certain extent. Ensuring the financial sustainability of the PNBA through BACoMaB remains an important objective for the EU (Appriou, 2016), in line with the CFP. This is motivated, in particular, by the multi-level governance set up by the trust fund to manage its endowment, allocate grants, and monitor and evaluate the activities of beneficiaries, which PNBA currently lacks (Appriou, 2016; Lefghih, 2016). In this context, a direct and unconditional allocation of funds to PNBA is difficult to justify before the EU Court of Auditors (Beddiyouh, 2016). BACoMaB recently took the initiative to address a request for direct funding to the EU and the Mauritanian Ministry of Fisheries, and they appear to have obtained positive feedback. This potential new channel to receiving funds from EU is currently being discussed (Appriou, 2016; Beddiyouh, 2016).

In Guinea-Bissau, the arrangement is more recent. Government commitments to the FBG trust fund remain *ad hoc*, and are not currently challenged, but concerns have been raised that it is now time for the trust fund to show that it can indeed support conservation activities. In this context, the French Global Environment Fund recently granted support to a set of pilot programmes to be run by the trust fund independently of its endowment. This initiative results from the hard lessons learned in Mauritania.

5.5. Challenges, opportunities and lessons learned

Both Mauritania and Guinea-Bissau have secured financial resources from FPAs with the EU to capitalise conservation trust funds that are intended to provide long-term and sustainable financing for the establishment and management of marine protected areas. These, in return, maintain the fishing potential of the surrounding seascapes, to the benefit of the EU fishing fleets. This arrangement can be considered an international payment for ecosystem services. From a political economy perspective, several lessons can be drawn from the experience of Mauritania and Guinea-Bissau.

Concerted lobbying efforts by environmental NGOs drove the establishment of the conservation trust funds

Putting such a system in place and ensuring it is maintained has revealed a number of challenges. Broad support must be established, which requires a shared understanding of the benefits that MPAs bring to the fishing sector and the benefits trust funds bring to marine conservation. In Mauritania and Guinea-Bissau, a well-established and credible "broker", namely FIBA, played a key role in establishing this consensus, through active lobbying and in the co-ordination of all those involved in country, in the EU, and in the broader donor community. IUCN also played an instrumental role in Guinea-Bissau, by laying the groundwork for broader institutional change concerning conservation. In addition, the continuous engagement by the World Bank was critical in enabling the FBG to be established and operationalised.

Substantial amounts of funding, well in excess of the immediate needs of the MPAs for maritime surveillance, created favorable enabling conditions, although competition for funds remains high. Shifts in EU policy, with growing concerns for more sustainable fishing practices, provided an important lever to convince national authorities to engage in the process. Aligning the interests of governments and the conservation community was essential to seize the opportunity offered by shifts in the EU's fisheries policy. Support from other donors (KfW, AFD, MAVA Foundation) was, in part, built on the demonstrable commitment of governments to engage in the process, and on the innovative character of the arrangement.

Wavering political support threatens long-term stability of financing arrangements

Once established, maintaining support for the arrangement can be difficult. In a context where governments' priorities have shifted away from conservation (resulting in fewer resources for sectoral support under the FPAs) and where lower interest rates challenge the rationale for placing funds in an endowment, it is unclear whether and how resources from FPAs will continue to support marine conservation.

In the case of BACoMaB in Mauritania, it seems that several years after the creation of the trust fund the government is not fully supportive of continuing to allocate a proportion of the funds received under the FPA for MPA conservation. The government is not naturally willing to earmark funds to an endowment aimed at securing long-term financing which could otherwise be used for short-term sectoral priorities.

FPAs and protocols are renegotiated on a regular basis, as are government budgets, which could jeopardise long-term commitments. Given these risks, it would be useful to ensure that conservation interests be represented in these negotiations, e.g. through the Ministry of Environment. The EU clearly has an important role to play in making support towards the conservation of marine biodiversity part of the negotiations.

Such uncertainties in the continued commitment of governments are one of the main justifications for establishing conservation trust funds in the first place, and the EU is now considering direct financing of trust funds in situations where it is supported by the partner country and is considered beneficial to ensuring its own goals (and financial management rules) under the CFP are met. It appears, however, that local support for conservation trust funds requires that they rapidly demonstrate their potential as actual grant-makers. Systematically associating revolving and sinking funds to endowments would help mitigate this perceived "taking-away" of scarce and valuable resources from short-term needs.

In the context of competition for scarce resource, securing benefits for the environment requires a strong legal basis

Policies and their reforms in the context of developing countries are often interrupted due to lack of funding or financing restrictions by donors. This undermines the achievements and progress made. Securing progress requires funding mechanisms that are financially and institutionally sustainable, such as conservation trust funds. However, securing the institutional framework underpinning the financial arrangement is equally important. In Mauritania, the capitalization of the endowment, based on an informal understanding, was rapidly challenged as leadership of partner institutions changed. This has jeopardised the partnership between the trust fund and the protected area authorities. A possible solution lies in making the trust fund an autonomous player, which can defend its role and interests, and establish a national constituency. The discussions that BACoMaB have initiated with the EU and the Mauritanian Ministry of Fisheries, independently of the PNBA and the Ministry of Environment, hint at the potential to enable the CTF to act as a new, independent, advocate for biodiversity.

Notes

1. The West African Marine Ecoregion spans Mauritania, Senegal, Cape Verde, The Gambia, Guinea-Bissau, Guinea and Sierra Leone (WWF, 2003).
2. Under the latest reform of the EU Common Fisheries Policy (CFP), which took effect on 1 January 2014, FPAs were renamed "Sustainable Fisheries Partnership Agreements".
3. Fleet access is negotiated to ensure that stocks are exploited in a sustainable manner, taking into account the precautionary and the Maximum Sustainable Yield approaches and favouring access priority of domestic fleets (European Commission, 2015). The FPAs intend to adhere to the FAO Code of Conduct for Responsible Fisheries through binding conditions for policy and management.
4. Fisheries access agreements are agreements between a coastal State and another State for the purpose of providing the fishing vessels of the latter with fishing opportunities in the waters of the former (Bartels et al., 2007). "Purely commercial agreement" refers to access to fisheries resources in exchange for financial compensation without any other concerns.
5. A quarter of catches by EU vessels is actually taking place in third country and international waters, reaching 90% for tuna and related species (European Parliament, 2015).
6. The Regulation 1006/2008 is also known as the Fishing Authorisation Regulation, which sets out rules regarding the access of third-country vessels to EU waters and the access of EU vessels to non-EU waters.
7. The debate on "sea-sharing" and "sea-sparing" refers to the question of sharing the oceans for co-management (allow human activities and nature to coexist by, for example, regulating fishing practices to maintain habitat quality over a larger area, so-called "sea-sharing") or sparing the oceans for fisheries and MPAs (e.g. concentrating conservation effort on the preservation of wild areas in no-take MPAs, and exploiting other areas for food production as intensively as we can, so-called "sea-sparing").
8. The conditionality criterion is not fully met as the payment to the MPAs, however, that the conditionality criteria is rarely met in PES, in particular when implemented in developing countries (Muradian et al., 2010).
9. In 2014, the FIBA was integrated into the MAVA Foundation, a private Swiss foundation.
10. The allocation is carried out by the Mauritanian Treasury, which receives the sectorial support allocation made by the EU.
11. In addition to fees paid by ship owners for licenses, paid directly to Mauritania, estimated at EUR 22 million per year (Official Journal of the EU, 2006).
12. Most CTFs are lodged out of the country to guarantee their independence and resilience to political shocks, etc. Risks of dissolution for CTFs lodged in the country are greater. The recent dissolution of the *Fondo Ambiental Nacional* of Ecuador offers a useful example. BACoMaB is under English Law and has a charitable organization status in UK with a host agreement allowing it to operate in Mauritania.
13. Since 2013, the new PNBA Director has refused to make this allocation to the BACoMaB.
14. Although the CFP reform officially came into effect on 1 January 2014, the implementation of new approaches began as early as 2012.
15. Mauritanian authorities, including the Prime Minister and the Ministry for Economy and Finance, are represented on the BACoMaB executive board.

References

Alder, J. and U.R. Sumaila (2004), "Western Africa: a fish basket of Europe past and present", *Journal of Environmental Development*, 13, 156-178, *http://dx.doi.org/10.1177/1070496504266092*.

Appriou, A. (2016), European External Action Service (EEAS) delegation in Mauritania, Interview on BACoMaB/BIOGUINE and fisheries agreements.

BACoMaB (2015), *Rapport annuel d'activités* [Annuel Activity Report].

Bartels, L. et al. (2007), *Policy Coherence for Development and the Effects of EU Fisheries Policies on Development in West Africa*, European Parliament, Directorate General External Policies of the Union.

Bastos, C. (2016), European External Action Service (EEAS) delegation in Guinea-Bissau, Interview on BACoMaB / BIOGUINE and fisheries agreements.

Beddiyouh, M. (2016), Agence Française de Développement (AFD) Mauritania, Interview on BACoMaB/ BIOGUINE and fisheries agreements.

Brown, K. (2005), "Addressing trade-offs in forest landscape restoration", in: *Forest Restoration in Landscapes*, Springer, New York, pp. 59–64.

Carr-Dirick, B. and U. Klug (2002), *Etude de faisabilité d'un fonds fiduciaire pour le Parc National du Banc d'Arguin* [Feasibility study of trust funds for the National Park of Banc d'Arguin].

Catry, P. et al. (2009), "Status, ecology, and conservation of sea turtles in Guinea-Bissau", *Chelonian Conserv. Biol.* 8, 150-160, *http://dx.doi.org/10.2744/CCB-0772.1*.

Catry, P. et al. (2002), "First census of the green turtle at Poilão, Bijagós Archipelago, Guinea-Bissau: The most important nesting colony on the Atlantic coast of Africa", *Oryx* 36, 400-403, *http://dx.doi.org/10.1017/S0030605302000765*.

Chavance, P. et al. (2004), "Pêcheries maritimes, écosystèmes et sociétés en Afrique de l'Ouest : un demi-siècle de changement" [Maritime fisheries, ecosystems and societies in West Africa : A half century of change], IRD Editions.

Chiron, G. (2016), Agence Française de Développement (AFD), Interview on BACoMaB/BIOGUINE and fisheries agreements.

COFREPECHE, MRAG, NFDS and POSEIDON, (2014), "Évaluations retrospectives et prospectives du protocole de l'accord de partenariat dans le secteur de la pêche entre l'Union européenne et la République islamique de Mauritanie" [Evaluation of the Protocol of the Fisheries Partnership Agreement between the European Union and Mauritania], Framework contrat MARE/2011/01 – Lot 3, specific contract number 8, Brussels.

Conservation Finance Alliance (CFA) (2008), "Revue des expériences des fonds fiduciaires pour la conservation de la biodiversité" [Review of experience with conservation trust funds for biodiversity], prepared for the CFA working group on environmental funds.

de Graaf, G. and L. Garibaldi, L. (2014), *The Value of African Fisheries*, FAO Fisheries and Aquaculture, Circular, No. 1093, Food and Agriculture Organisation of the United Nations, Rome.

Diop, S. and P.A. Scheren (2016), "Sustainable oceans and coasts: lessons learnt from Eastern and Western Africa", *Estuar. Coast. Shelf Sci.*, *http://dx.doi.org/10.1016/j.ecss.2016.03.032*.

Engelmoer, M. et al. (1984), "The Banc d'Arguin (Mauritania)" in: Evans, P.R., J.D. Goss-Custard and W.G. Hale (Eds.), *Coastal Waders and Wildfowl in Winter*, Cambridge, pp. 293-310.

European Commission (EC) (2015), "EU SFPAs: Sustainable Fisheries Partnership Agreements", *http://ec.europa.eu/fisheries/documentation/publications/2015-sfpa_en.pdf* (accessed 6 September 2016).

European Commission (EC) (2007), EU report on policy coherence for development, No. 545 final, *Commission Working Paper*.

European Court of Auditors (2015), "Are the Fisheries Partnership Agreements well managed by the Commission?", Special report, No. 11, *www.eca.europa.eu/Lists/ECADocuments/SR15_11/SR_FISHERIES_EN.pdf* (accessed 6 September 2016).

European Parliament (2015), *Council Regulation 1006/2008 on Fishing Authorisations: Implementation Appraisal*.

Failler, P. (2006), *Impact of Trade-linked Policies on the Management of Fisheries in West Africa*, IIFET 2006 Portsmouth Proceedings.

Food and Agriculture Organisation of the United Nations (FAO), (2011), *Review of the State of World Marine Fishery Resources, FAO Fisheries and Aquaculture Technical Paper* 569.

Food and Agriculture Organisation of the United Nations (FAO), (2009), *The State of World Fisheries and Aquaculture 2008*, Food and Agriculture Organisation of the United Nations, Rome.

Garcia, S.M. et al. (2013), "Les aires marines protégées et la pêche : bioécologie, socioéconomie et gouvernance", [Marine protected areas and fishing], Presses Universitaires de Perpignan, Perpignan.

GEF Secretariat (1998), *Evaluation of Experience with Conservative Trust Funds*, GEF Evaluation Office.

Goyet, S. (2016), Fondation Internationale du Banc d'Arguin [International Foundation of the Banc d'Arguin] (FIBA), Interview on BACoMaB / BIOGUINE and fisheries agreements.

Guénette, S. et al. (2014), "Assessing the contribution of marine protected areas to the trophic functioning of ecosystems: a model for the Banc d'Arguin and the Mauritanian Shelf", *PLOS ONE* 9, e94742, *http://dx.doi.org/10.1371/journal.pone.0094742*.

Hogan, R. (2003), "Environmentalists target EU access agreement", *Science in Africa*.

Institute for European Environmental Policy (IEEP) (2002), "Fisheries agreements with third countries – is the EU moving towards sustainable development?", *www.ieep.eu/publications/2002/11/fisheries-agreements-with-third-countries-is-the-eu-moving-towards-sustainable-development* (accessed 10 August 2016).

International Union for Conservation of Nature (IUCN) (2003), *Stratégie régionale pour les aires marines protégées en Afrique de l'Ouest,* [Regional Strategy for Marine Protected Areas in West Africa], IUCN, WWF, FIBA, Wetlands International.

Lefghih, A. (2016), BACoMaB Trust Fund, Interview on BACoMaB/BIOGUINE and fisheries agreements.

Matthew, S. (2003), "Small-scale fisheries perspectives on an ecosystem-based approach to fisheries management", in *Responsible Fisheries in the Marine Ecosystem*, Sinclair and Valdimarsson (Eds.), Food and Agriculture Organisation of the United Nations, CABI Publishing.

Muradian, R. et al. (2010), "Reconciling theory and practice: An alternative conceptual framework for understanding payments for environmental services", *Ecol. Econ.*, Special Section – Payments for Environmental Services: Reconciling Theory and Practice 69, 1202-1208, *http://dx.doi.org/10.1016/j.ecolecon.2009.11.006*.

Oceana (2011), *The European Union and Fishing Subsidies*, *http://eu.oceana.org/sites/default/files/reports/Oceana_EU_Subsidy_Report.pdf* (accessed 8 August 2016).

OECD (2017 *forthcoming*), *Marine Protected Areas: Economics, Management and Good Practice Insights*, OECD Publishing, Paris.

Official Journal of the European Union (2014), *Protocol setting out the fishing opportunities and financial contribution provided for in the Fisheries Partnership Agreement between the European Community and the Republic of Guinea-Bissau*, 13 November 2014, *http://eur-lex.europa.eu/legal-content/EN/TXT/PDF/?uri=CELEX:22014A1113(01)&qid=1416916918243&from=EN* (accessed 7 September 2016).

Official Journal of the European Union (2012), *Protocol setting out the fishing opportunities and financial contribution provided for in the Fisheries Partnership Agreement between the European Union and the Islamic Republic of Mauritania for a period of two years*, 31 December 2012, *http://eur-lex.europa.eu/LexUriServ/LexUriServ.do?uri=OJ:L:2012:361:0043:0084:EN:PDF* (accessed 7 September 2016).

Official Journal of the European Union (2008), *Protocol setting out the fishing opportunities and financial contribution provided for in the Fisheries Partnership Agreement between the European Community and the Islamic Republic of Mauritania for the period 1 August 2008 to 31 July 2012*, 31 July 2008, *http://www2.ecolex.org/server2neu.php/libcat/docs/TRE/Full/Other/TRE-151488.pdf* (accessed 7 September 2016).

Official Journal of the European Union (2007), *Fisheries Partnership Agreement between the European Community and the Republic of Guinea-Bissau for the period 16 June 2007 to 15 June 2011*, 27 December 2011, *http://eur-lex.europa.eu/resource.html?uri=cellar:55fa6af9-2f96-4998-9669-1f7455b92b00.0006.01/DOC_3&format=PDF* (accessed 7 September 2016).

Official Journal of the European Union (2006), *Fisheries Partnership Agreement between the European Community and the Islamic Republic of Mauritania*, Official Journal of the European Union, 8 December 2006, *http://eur-lex.europa.eu/resource.html?uri=cellar:2366ed9d-4b10-4d83-8406-4e51476f7e27.0005.02/DOC_2&format=PDF* (accessed 7 September 2016).

Ould Ahmed Salem, Z. (2012), "Les écueils du "partenariat": l'Union européenne et les accords de pêche avec l'Afrique" [The pitfalls of "partnership": The European Union and the fisheries agreements with Africa], *Polit. Afr.* 23-42.

Renaud, T. (2016), MAVA Foundation, Interview on BACoMaB/BIOGUINE and fisheries agreements.

Roberts, C. et al. (2002), "Marine Biodiversity Hotspots and Conservation Priorities for Tropical Reefs", *Science*, Vol 295.

Spergel, B. and M. Moye (2004), *Financing Marine Conservation: A Menu of Options*, WWF, Center for Conservation Finance, Washington, DC.

UNEP-WCMC, (2008), *National and Regional Networks of Marine Protected Areas: A Review of Progress*, *www.unep.org/regionalseas/publications/otherpubs/pdfs/MPA_Network_report.pdf* (accessed 8 August 2016).

West African Sustainable Seafood Development Alliance (WASSDA) (2008), *West African Fisheries Profile*, *www.imcsnet.org/imcs/docs/west_africa_fisheries_country_profile_exec_sum.pdf* (accessed 15 August 2016).

Wolff et al. (1993), "The functioning of the ecosystem of the Banc d'Arguin, Mauritania: A review", *Hydrobiologia* 258, 211-222, *http://dx.doi.org/10.1007/BF00006198*.

Wunder, S. (2015), "Revisiting the concept of payments for environmental services", *Ecol. Econ.* 117, 234-243, *http://dx.doi.org/10.1016/j.ecolecon.2014.08.016*.

WWF Wamer and Wetlands International (2007), "Plan de Suivi et de Conservation de l'Écorégion Littoral de l'Afrique de l'Ouest", [Action Plan for the Conservation of the Coastal Ecoregion in West Africa].

Yudelman, T. (2016), Consultant to The World Bank, Interview on BACoMaB/BIOGUINE and fisheries agreements. 16/06/2016.

The Political Economy of Biodiversity Policy Reform

Chapter 6

The political economy of the ITQ system and resource rent tax in Icelandic fisheries

This case examines the political economy of the reform to establish an economically efficient and more environmentally-sustainable fisheries management system in Iceland based on individually transferable quotas. It also discusses the introduction of a resource rent tax to more broadly share the benefits from harvesting a common property resource with the general public. The case study draws lessons learned about the drivers of reform, how distributional issues were addressed, and how subsequent reforms were undertaken to respond to specific stakeholder demands.

Introduction

The introduction in the 1980s of the individually transferrable quota (ITQ) management system in the Icelandic fisheries was driven by a looming crisis. It became apparent that the status quo would most likely lead to fisheries collapse and major economic hardships for the country as a whole. With the Fisheries Act in 1990, the ITQ system became comprehensive and thus, the cornerstone of the fisheries management system. Evidence suggests that the Icelandic ITQ system has been very successful in increasing efficiency in the fisheries and created the correct incentives for fishers when it comes to safeguarding and rebuilding fish stocks. The case study shows how a crisis threatening an economically vital industry can provide the political drive for reform. It also illustrates that despite the overall economic gains of the reform, it still produced winners and losers, which spurred later reforms to the system.

6.1. An overview of marine biodiversity and the fisheries sector in Iceland

Marine biodiversity in Iceland

Around 270 fish species have been identified in Icelandic marine waters and at least 150 of these spawn within the exclusive economic zone (EEZ). Only around 20 of these are harvested to any considerable extent by the fishing fleet and just a handful of species (notably cod) predominate in catches (MENR, 2014). The warm and cold currents in Icelandic seas combined with nutrient-rich seawater provide an environment highly conducive to flourishing marine life and high-yield fishing grounds. Although measurable amounts of pollutants are found in marine catches, pollutant concentrations in fish are generally below maximum levels and declining, which is important for maintaining the market value of Icelandic marine produce (MENR, 2014). This productive marine ecosystem has supported a robust fishing industry, accounting for about 7% of GDP, with marine products representing more than 25% of total exports of goods and services in 2012 (measured in value); although the share has been in decline since 2000 (OECD, 2014).

Iceland's first National Biodiversity Strategy (NBS) was prepared by the Ministry of Environment and Natural Resources (MENR) and adopted by the Government in 2008. An Action Plan for the implementation of the NBS was prepared by the Ministry for the Environment, in co-operation with other relevant ministries, and approved by the Government in 2010. The main focus is on increasing knowledge about the state and trend of biological diversity and securing protection of species in danger or threatened by extinction. Although fisheries do not figure prominently in the NBS, Iceland has designated five protected areas for the conservation of cold water corals as well as three marine areas protected for biological diversity, with a total of 455 000 hectares of marine protected areas (MENR, 2014).

Iceland's National Strategy for Sustainable Development includes specific objectives related to the sustainable use of living marine resources (MENR, 2010). The objectives emphasise that the use of fish stocks should remain on a sustainable basis and based on the best available scientific findings. They also state that for those fishing stocks that require harvest limits, a cautionary approach to management should be taken, so as to achieve maximum yields over the long run. Finally, the objectives specify that the use of living marine resources should take into account the diverse interplay of the marine ecosystem and should aim to minimise negative effects of the use on other parts of the ecosystems. In the context of pollution prevention, the Strategy also includes an objective stating that the concentration of man-made pollutants in Icelandic marine products should always be less than the strictest standards of domestic and foreign health authorities (MENR, 2010).

Currently, none of the commercially harvested species in Iceland are considered to be threatened due to overfishing, although non-sustainable exploitation has been a problem in the past (MENR, 2014). For example, in the late 1960s, herring populations collapsed due to over-fishing and a drop in seawater temperatures, but have since recovered. For demersal fish,[1] cod has experienced considerable declines, although haddock has increased. For many years, demersal fish catches exceeded levels recommended by scientists, but over the past decade, the limit of total allowable catches has been in line with the advice of the Marine Research Institute.[2] The main purpose of most of the marine fisheries management areas has been to secure the sustainable use of the harvested resources, but not necessarily to conserve biological diversity *per se* (MENR, 2014).

Development of the fisheries sector in Iceland

For many centuries, foreign fishing fleets were prevalent off the coast of Iceland. The first half of the twentieth century was marked by the struggle of Icelanders to control their waters and secure exclusive access to the resources. In 1901 Iceland declared a fishing limit of three nautical miles, which was extended to four miles in 1952. The fishing limits were gradually extended, to 12 miles, 50 miles and 200 miles in 1958, 1972 and 1976, respectively resulting in significant declines of foreign catches in Icelandic waters (Figure 6.1). These extensions were all opposed at the time by other fishing nations that used to fish in these

Figure 6.1. **Declining foreign catches of cod in Icelandic waters**

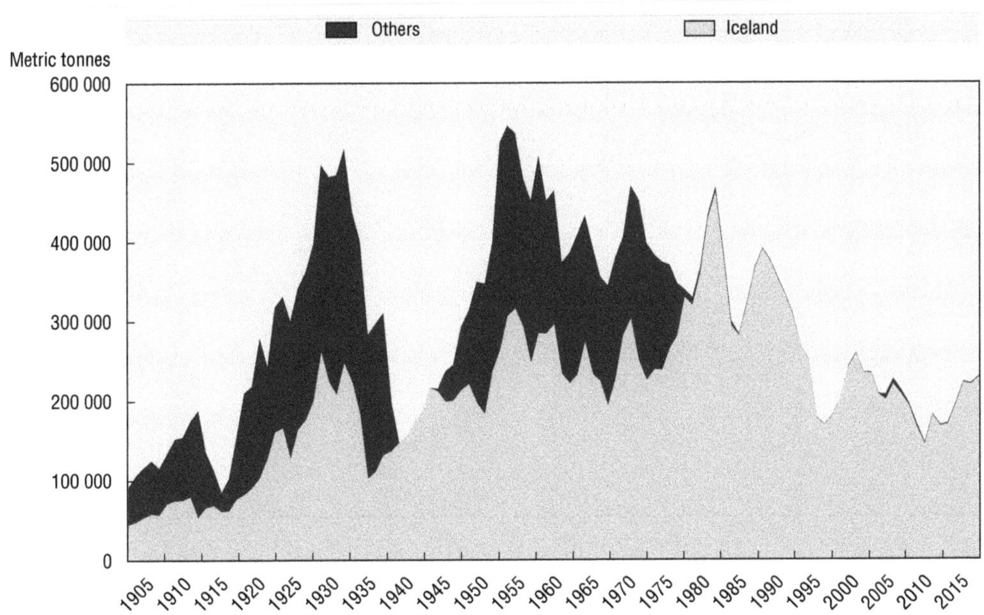

Source: Based on data from Marine Research Institute (2016), *http://data.hafro.is/assmt/2016/cod/*.

waters, but these disputes have since been resolved by international agreements.[3] The reasons behind the willingness of Icelanders to fend off foreigners were many, and included conservation issues such as the perceived danger of damaging coastal fishing grounds with the use of trawls and overfishing (Jóhannesson, 2004).

Year-round fishing villages did not appear around the Icelandic coast until the industrialisation of fisheries in the early twentieth-century[4] when fisheries finally took off, quickly becoming the backbone of the economy.[5] Although the share of the fishing industry in the economy, and notably as a percentage of the total labour force, has decreased over the years, it is still vital to Iceland's prosperity and it is still the most important industry in many of the rural regions (Figure 6.2).

Figure 6.2. **Fishing industry's share of GDP and total labour force**

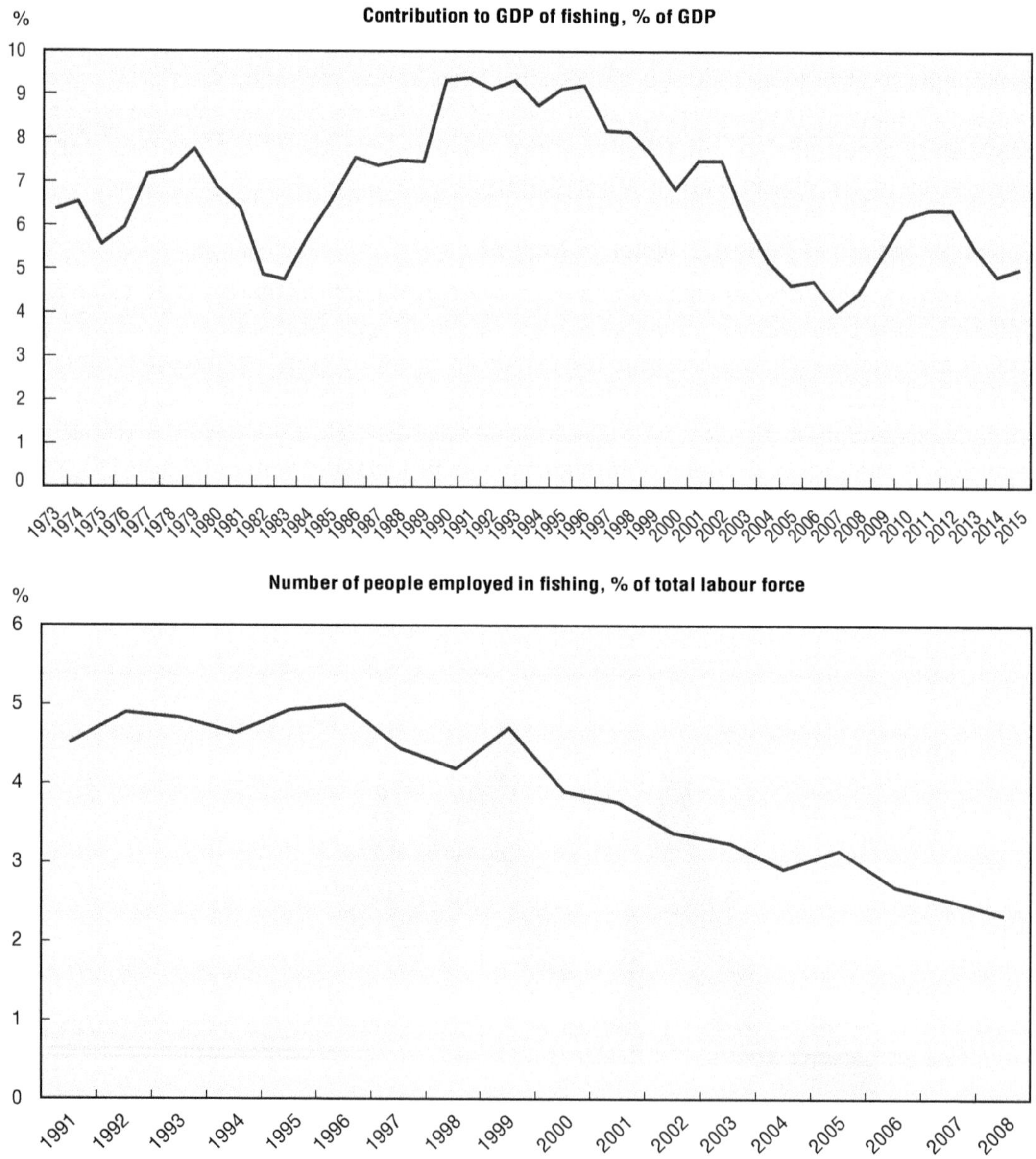

Source: Based on data from Statistic Iceland (2016), personal correspondence with G. Thordardottir.

The economic importance of fishing to the overall economy hinges upon many factors, both related to the industry itself, such as fishability and abundance of different species, but also the macroeconomic situation in general, not least the exchange rate of the local currency. Although the relative importance of the fishing industry in the Icelandic economy has declined (notably as a percentage of the total labour force), it still is one of the mainstays of the economy, accounting for 5% of GDP in 2015 (Figure 6.2). Around 56.7% of total merchandise export value came from seafood exports in 2015 (Statistics Iceland, author's calculations).

In many rural regions, fishing is still the most important industry. It is notable that Iceland has a population of around 330 000 inhabitants of which around two-thirds live in the Southwest of the country, including the capital Reykjavik. The remaining population lives in scattered villages along the coast and on farms. In the fishing villages, there used to be very few opportunities outside of the fishing industry, until the beginning of the current boom in the tourism industry.

6.2. The introduction and evolution of the ITQ system

As is the case with many reforms, the introduction of the ITQ management system in the Icelandic fisheries was driven by a looming crisis. Fishing in Iceland expanded considerably in the post-war period,[6] with foreign fishing fleets returning with an ever-increasing fishing effort due to technological advances and a considerable increase in the size of the Icelandic fleet. Catches of some valuable species such as haddock, decreased sharply between 1949 and 1953 and scientists became concerned about the state of some of the commercially important stocks. In 1975, the Marine Resource Institute published a report warning that if the cod fisheries were to be continued in a similar way, the catches were bound to fall drastically, mostly due to overfishing (Hafrannsóknastofnun, 1975). Due to its bleak message, the report was colloquially referred to as "The Black Report". The main indications were poor recruitment and a diminishing size of fishable stock (Jakobsson, 1979). To manage the fishery, various effort restrictions were dominant (days-at-sea limitations and gear restrictions) and setting of total allowable catches (TACs) for different species.

Contrary to the prevailing belief at the time, good management was not secured by imposing gear and effort restrictions, setting TACs, providing subsidies to scrap fishing vessels or driving foreign fishing fleets from Icelandic waters.[7] Since the common-property nature of the resource remained, the fishery consequently continued to suffer from overexploitation. It became apparent that Icelanders themselves had increased their fishing fleets and effort beyond what was biologically sustainable and that the economic performance of the fishing industry was poor as a result (Danielsson, 1997). Total productivity in the fishing industry (following the ITQ reforms) was 73% higher in 1995 than in 1973, compared to an increase in total productivity in other industries (excluding fish processing) of 21% over the same period (National Economic Institute, 1999). Emphasis had been on increasing investments in the fishing fleet to generate jobs and support rural regions depending on fisheries often with financial support through state-owned funds (Schrank, 2003; Matthiasson, 2008). Furthermore, although the Marine Resource Institute regularly published results regarding the recommended TAC for the main species, ministerial decisions by the Minister of Fisheries on the TAC most often exceeded the recommendations due to political and economic pressures from the electorate and the industry respectively, resulting in higher actual landings (Figure 6.3). Deviations from scientific recommendation was justified by referring to the uncertainty of scientific evidence and the economic and social necessity of not decreasing catches too dramatically in order to safeguard employment.

Figure 6.3. **Narrowing discrepancy between the recommended TAC for cod and landings, 1995-2015**

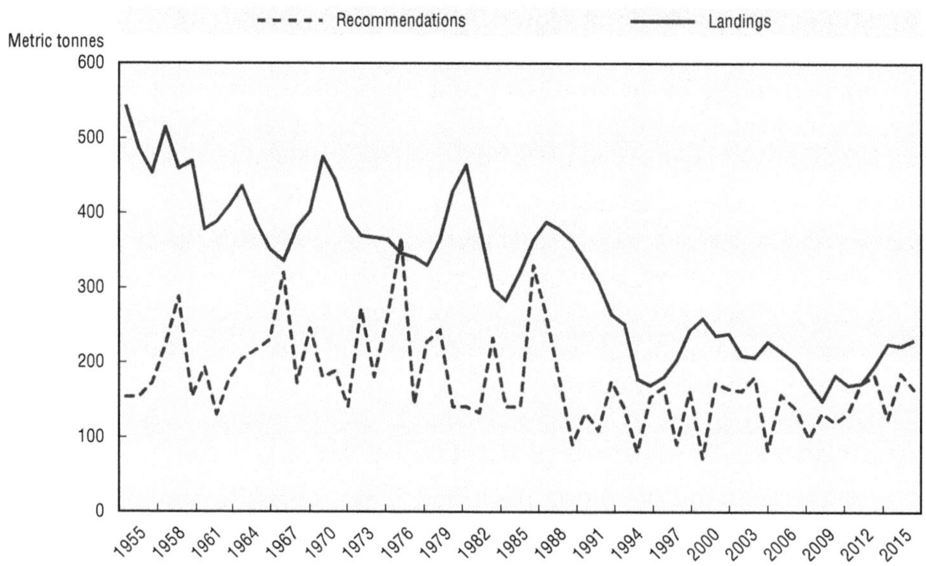

Source: Based on data from Marine Research Institute (2016), *http://data.hafro.is/*.

The Black Report underlined the need for reform and a new Black Report was released in 1983. It became apparent that the status quo would most likely lead to disaster and, given the importance of the fisheries for the national economy, that was not a gamble that many were willing to take, as a collapse of the fisheries would most certainly lead to major economic hardships for the country as a whole. A formal analysis of the mechanism leading up to the reforms is lacking but, generally speaking, the aforementioned poor economic performance of the fisheries coupled with scientific evidence on the poor state of commercially important stocks finally pushed the parliament to introduce new management measures.

Finally, in 1984 the ITQ system was introduced in the demersal fisheries with the allocation of the first quotas allotted to vessels. Individual quota systems (some transferable, others non-transferable) had already been used in some pelagic fisheries (herring and capelin) from the 1970s, and had proven to be very successful in reducing fleet sizes and fishing effort. With little doubt it can be said that this positive experience in Iceland helped in the introduction of a quota system in the more important demersal fisheries. Nevertheless, it was not self-evident that this positive experience from the pelagic fisheries could be applied to the more economically and socially important demersal fisheries.

This reform process was primarily driven by scientists, politicians and public servants. The involvement with other stakeholders, such as industry leaders and trade unions, was minimal. When the ITQ system was first introduced, it was not specified whether the new system was permanent or temporary. It was also clear that as with most reforms there would be winners and losers. As discussed later, not everyone participated in the ITQ system from the beginning and because the success of the system was not guaranteed, it would be an oversimplification to say that even all incumbents were supportive of the system in the beginning.[8]

The ITQ system was gradually introduced into Icelandic fisheries, incorporating more and more species and with more clear rules on transferability. It was nevertheless difficult to ensure that the TAC was not exceeded, partly because some boats could still opt for effort restrictions instead of quotas. Finally, with a new Fisheries Act in 1990, the ITQ system became comprehensive and thus, the cornerstone of the fisheries management system.

The essential feature of the ITQ system is that the quotas represent defined shares in the TAC of given stocks each fishing year. The quotas are permanent, perfectly divisible and fairly freely transferable. Discarding of fish is prohibited as well as high-grading. The TAC for each fishing season is formally decided upon by the Minister of Fisheries and is based on the scientific recommendation of the Marine Resource Institute. The allotted TAC for each species has followed quite closely the scientific recommendations in recent years. Since the fishing year 1994-95, specific catch rules have been used in determining the recommended TAC for cod. These catch rules, which basically set the allowable TAC for cod as a percentage of fishable stock size, were set to rebuild the spawning stock while at the same time providing clear guidance to industry on how that would be achieved.[9]

Has the ITQ system been a success?

From a pure economic theory point of view property rights-based systems in fisheries, if designed and implemented correctly, should yield numerous economic benefits, including;[10]

- Reduced fishing effort due to the elimination of competition between vessels
- Reduced cost of effort as firms can focus on catching their share with the lowest costs
- Improved quality of catch as the firms are restricted by the quotas and can only increase revenue by improving the quality of catches
- Reduction in fleet size due to rationalisation through buying and selling of quotas (less efficient vessels sell quotas and opt out of the fishery
- Rent generation

There is ample evidence to support the view that the Icelandic ITQ system has been very successful in increasing efficiency in the fisheries. Overcapitalization, in the form of too large a fleet, unravelled quickly and profitability increased (Figure 6.4). The former situation of the fishing fleet being a recipient of state-aid quickly became history.[11] Although direct subsidies in the Icelandic fisheries were generally lower than in many other countries, various programmes existed, e.g. public investments funds, funds granting fuel subsidies, vessel buyback programs and export grants. Also, before the ITQ system, the exchange rate of the national currency rate was regularly adjusted to improve the competitiveness of the fish exports compared to the main foreign competitors.[12]

Given the option for smaller vessels to stay outside of the ITQ system, their numbers increased at the same time as larger boats exited the fishery (Figure 6.5).

It is more difficult to evaluate the biological success of the system because of the inherent complexity and dynamics of the ecological system. However, it is clear that the reduction in fishing effort has secured the sustainability of most of the commercially exploited species (Figure 6.6).

There are two important points to keep in mind when evaluating the biological and economic successes of the ITQ system in Iceland. First, the reduction in fishing effort was made possible due to the ITQ system. While it was necessary to reduce TACs for many species, notably cod, the fishers received quota shares in return, which helped them to survive the consequent economic hardships. The less efficient vessels could exit the fishery and were compensated through the sale of their quota shares.

Figure 6.4. **Significant consolidation of the Icelandic fishing fleet led to higher profitability**

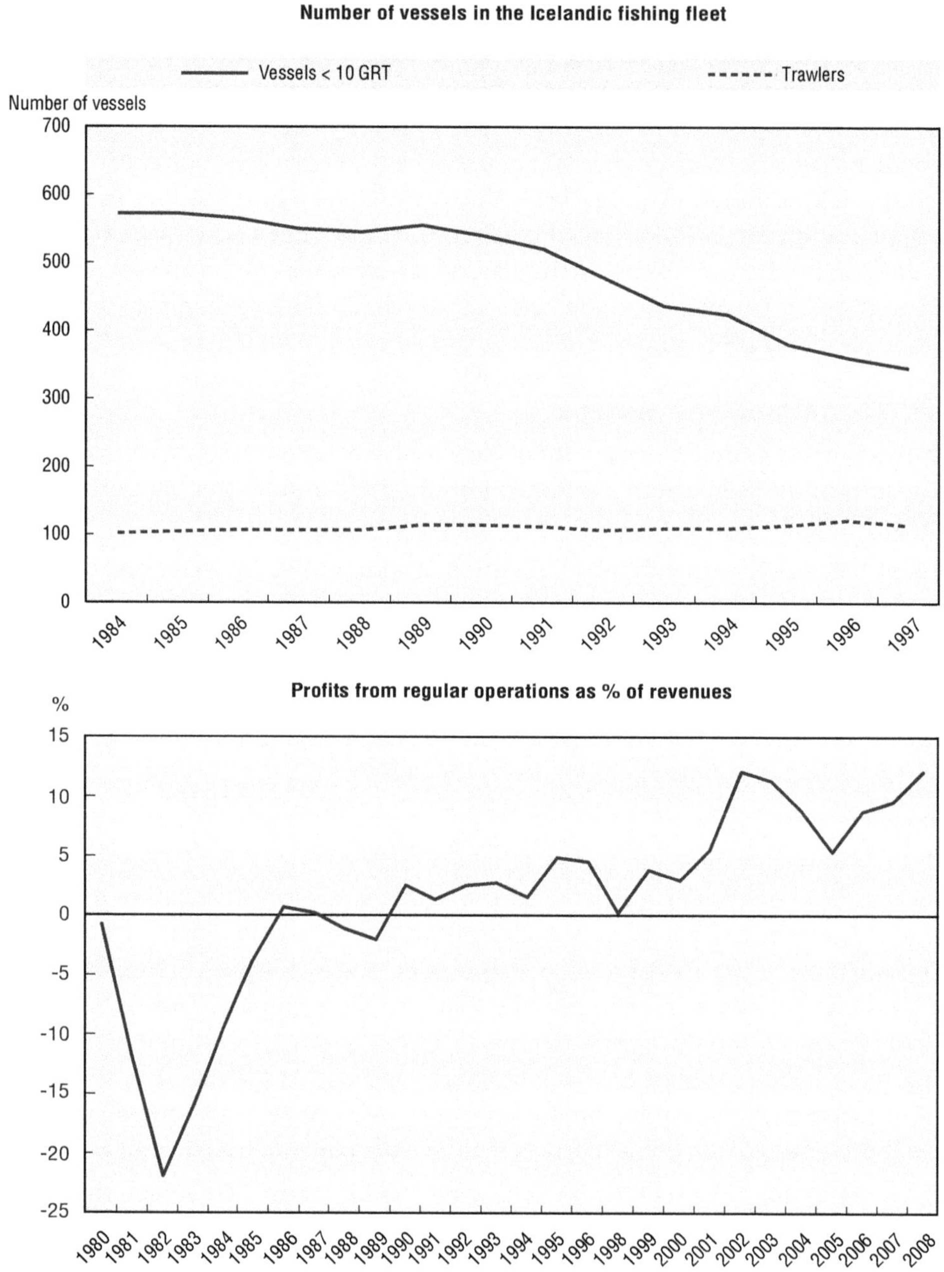

Note: GRT= "gross registered tonnes".
Source: Based on data from Statistic Iceland (2016), personal correspondence with G. Thordardottir.

Second, property rights systems such as ITQs can create the correct incentives for fishers when it comes to safeguarding and rebuilding fish stocks.[13] Those that have permanent quota shares are able to take a long-term perspective as secure access rights mean that they can have confidence in being able to reap the benefits of fishing less today if restricting fishing now will increase their chances of fishing more later.[14] This is of utmost importance as the appropriate incentive structure eliminates the wasteful race-to-fish

Figure 6.5. **The number of smaller vessels increased, then declined**

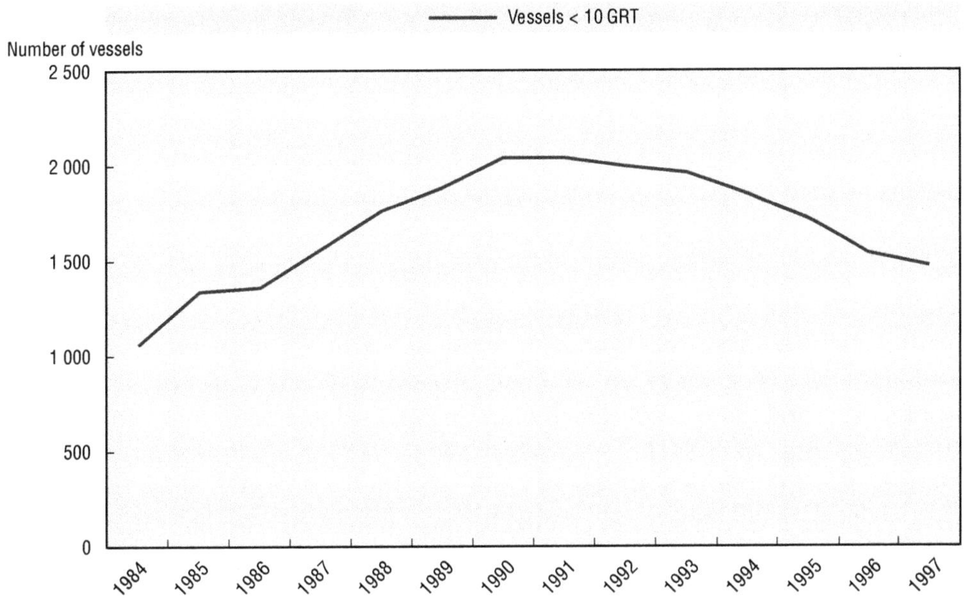

Source: Based on data from Statistic Iceland (2016), personal correspondence with G. Thordardottir.

Figure 6.6. **Trends in spawning stock biomass for cod**

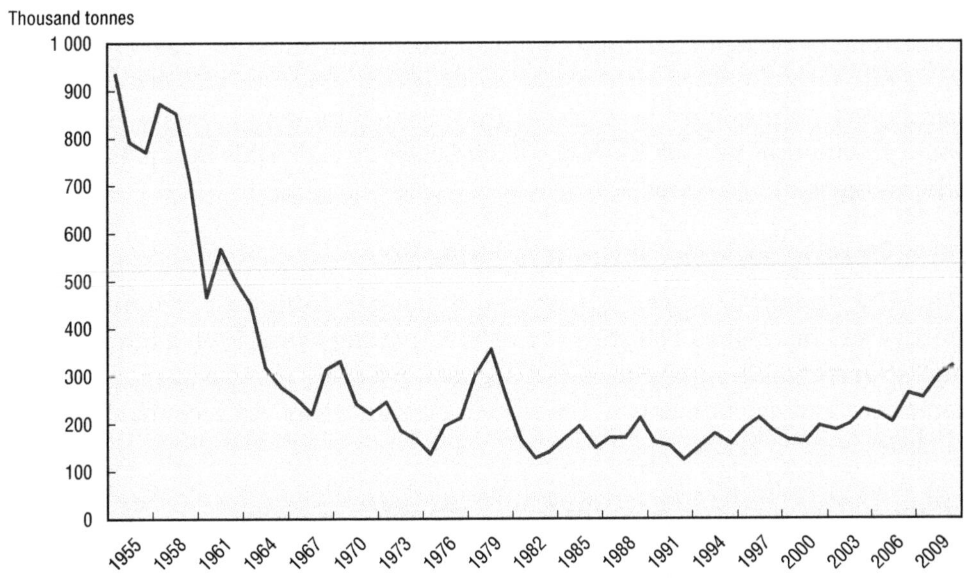

Source: Based on data from Marine Resource Institute (2016), *http://data.hafro.is/assmt/2016/cod/*.

and the so-called "Tragedy of the Commons", which has often proven to be devastating for the biological sustainability of fish resources.[15] The Fisheries Directorate keeps track of all exchanges between vessels by prices and quantities for each species. One measure of the economic efficiency of the ITQ system is to look at quota values over time. The annual quota rental values in the Icelandic fisheries increased dramatically (around 20-fold) between 1984 and 1999.[16]

The fisheries management system and biodiversity

The Icelandic ITQ system was a major reform driven mainly by economic considerations spurred by the threat of collapse of the most important fish stock. Given the economic importance of the fisheries, it was politically acceptable to adopt such drastic measures. When the system was introduced, the focus was mainly on avoiding collapse and improving overall economic performance in the sector, by dramatically decreasing fishing effort. Biodiversity as such, was not high on the agenda.

ITQ systems create incentives for fishers to operate in an economically efficient manner. Being assured a predefined share of the harvest provides surety and reduces the wasteful need to race, whilst transferability of quota brings market forces to bear on fishers by creating financial incentives to maximise the net return they generate on their quota. From a biodiversity perspective, an associated benefit of ITQs is that if the TAC is set at an appropriate level and there is effective monitoring and enforcement, they can also result in sustainable exploitation of the fish stocks they are used to manage. However, as the focus of ITQs is typically limited to a subset of commercially exploited species their ability to conserve biodiversity in the broader context is constrained by the scope of their application. When it comes to limiting the overall effects of fishing on biodiversity, other measures in addition to TACs for different species are needed.[17]

For these reasons, traditional management measures that protect habitat and reproduction capabilities in the ecosystem have always been applied along with the ITQ system in Iceland. These measures include temporal closures of spawning grounds, temporal spatial closures to protect juveniles, as well as restrictions on gear types for different time periods and fishing grounds. Such measures are based on scientific recommendations provided by the Marine Research Institute and are implemented frequently. Some zones have been closed from fishing for many years while others are closed for shorter time periods. The Coast Guard plays an active role in surveillance related to such management measures.

6.3. Political economy aspects of the ITQ system

The ITQ system has been considered a success from an economic efficiency perspective and has helped fish stocks to recover, putting fisheries on a more sustainable footing. However, political tensions and discontent have still emerged, spurring a number of exemptions and amendments to the system over the years. An account of some of the major issues is given below.

Distributional issues arose from the initial allocation of quotas

Much of the political discontent is due to the initial allocation of the quotas.[18] When the system was first implemented for the demersal fisheries in 1984, the quotas were allocated to vessels based on each vessel's average share in the total catch in the three years prior, i.e. 1981-83. There were certain exceptions to this rule, such as if the vessel in question had not been in full operation, e.g. because of major repairs or having entered the fishery later than 1981, the share was adjusted upwards. In the years 1985-87, there was a possibility to modify the TAC shares by temporarily opting for effort restrictions instead of quotas and thereby demonstrating higher catches during this period. When the allocations were made it was not stipulated whether they were permanent or not. From a legal standpoint, the quota shares represent user rights rather than property rights to the resource as such.

This approach, of initially grandfathering fishing rights is very common for property rights based systems because it is often the easiest approach from a political perspective and it can have positive efficiency advantages compared to some other means of distribution, e.g. by increasing rents by raising expected rates of return for investment and lowering the cost of capital.[19] However, even more than thirty years later, this is considered by some people in and outside the industry to have been an unjust way of disbursing rights to harvest a commonly owned resource.[20] According to the Fisheries Act, fish resources in Icelandic waters are common property of the nation, but the right to harvest has been transferred to the quota owners.

Whatever position one may have on the fairness of initially distributing fishing rights through a grandfathering system, it would be almost impossible to undo the distributional effects of the initial allocation now, as the quotas have been bought and sold many times over since the initial allocation and many of the vessel owners that received quotas originally have left the industry. The quota market is quite competitive and there is clear evidence of concentration of quotas with increasing transfers between different harbours (Agnarsson, et al., 2016). Through the Fisheries Act there is a limit to how much of the total quota for each species a company (or related businesses) can own.

A related issue to the initial allocation debate is how the general public in Iceland should receive benefits from the commonly owned fish resources. Although it is undeniable that the Icelandic economy has benefitted greatly from a more efficient fishing industry, claims have been made that the ITQ system generates resource rents to companies in the industry and that these resource rents should to a greater extent, accrue to the general public.[21] Such claims have been voiced by different people and groups, including scholars and politicians. It is difficult to pinpoint such claims to specific political parties or views, or specific stakeholders. Regional differences exist when it comes to different views regarding critique of the system (Kokorsch et al., 2015). Since the introduction of the ITQ system most political parties in Iceland have taken part in various coalition governments, but all governments have kept the fundamentals of the system in place with only marginal changes made to the system. We give an overview of the most important ones below.[22]

A resource rent tax sought to remedy some of the distributional issues related to the initial free allocation of quotas

The Icelandic fishing firms have paid special fishing fees, mainly used to finance the running of the fisheries management system, since 2001. In 2012 a special resource rent tax was introduced. This resource tax is two-fold, i.e. it is composed of a general part, which replaced the older fishing fees and a specific part which is aimed at collecting a part of the resource rent. The resource rent tax system is quite complicated and has evolved over time but essentially it takes into consideration the profit margin in the harvesting of different species.[23] Fundamentally, the system is designed in such a way that the different variable cost of fishing different species is reflected in the species specific tax rates.

The total tax receipts from this tax have changed somewhat over the years, due to changes in the profitability of the different fisheries over time. The tax levied on the industry amounted to ISK 12.8 billion for the fishing year 2012/13 and ISK 7.7 billion for the fishing year 2014/15.[24] To put this into perspective, net profits of fishing firms (EBT) amounted to ISK 14.8 billion in 2014 and total tax receipts from Icelandic firms (tax on revenue and profits) amounted to roughly ISK 58.6 billion in 2015 (Statistics Iceland, 2014; Fjársýsla ríkisins, 2016). The revenues from the resource rent tax accrue to the general government budget.

Even though the resource rent tax has provided increased revenues to the state, there is still discussion on whether the tax rate is set too high or too low. Furthermore, in spite of the introduction of the resource rent tax, there are still claims for using other methods to collect the resource rent into the state coffers, such as through the auctioning of the fishing rights by the government. The main rationale being that an auctioning mechanism would reveal the true monetary value of the right in a better way than the current system. The fact that the Icelandic fishing industry can pay a special resource rent tax on top of other taxes and at the same time receives no subsidies, can be seen as a sign of its economic efficiency.

Exemptions for small vessels aimed to protect rural employment, but undermined the sustainability of the system

Although the Icelandic ITQ system was quite uniform from the start, the smallest boats in the fleet were exempt from the system in the beginning. The small vessel fleet is driven by professional motives rather than for subsistence or leisure, but is considered to create employment in many rural areas. Due to political desire to conserve employment in rural fishing villages there was a tendency to safeguard this fleet from consolidation through quota trades. In 1984, all boats measuring less than 10 gross registered tons were allotted 3.77% of the total cod catch of each year, but no restrictions were put on effort or catches for individual boats. The Ministry of Fisheries was supposed to stop the fishing activity of this fleet if the TAC was exceeded. This was not done despite exceedance of the TAC in both 1984 and 1985 due to political pressure from small scale fishers and rural communities, which were dependent on employment linked to small scale fishing.

In the years that followed, the authorities used various measures to try to get these small vessels to exit various effort-control regimes and enter the general ITQ system in spite of the aforementioned political resistance. The main driver behind this willingness to incorporate the small vessels in an ITQ system was to increase the overall efficiency of the industry, while political resistance came from those who stressed the importance of the small vessel fleet in maintaining rural employment. When various amendments were made to the Fishing Act in 1988-90 the legislative body tried to limit the increase in the number of small fishing vessels, which were entering the fishery. Nevertheless, new boats entered the fishery through various means often replacing those that exited.

The catches of this fleet were substantial. In the fishing year 1994/95, around 35% of the total cod catches in Iceland accrued to this fleet. In the fishing year 2001/02 the share of the small vessel fleet in the total catch of cod was around 8%, although the number of vessels had been reduced substantially. The number of small vessels outside the ITQ system was 1 022 in the fishing year 1993/94 but was down to 293 in the fishing year 2002/03.[25]

After various twists and turns aimed at reducing the fishing effort of the small vessel system which remained outside the ITQ system, the Minister of Fisheries finally decided in 2004 to abort the days-at-sea regime option for small boats and required them to enter an ITQ system. At that time, the number of small vessels outside of the system had decreased as previously discussed and the political resistance had diminished accordingly.

This development clearly shows the complicated political economy issues that can arise in fisheries reforms where different fleet segments are not treated in the same way. For example, it can be argued that in a situation where some fleet segments are exempt from being managed under an ITQ system they have an incentive to free-ride when it comes to rebuilding fish stocks.[26] This hinges upon the assumption that such stakeholders have the political clout to do so.

Regional quotas were put in place to support communities where fishing is an economic mainstay

The transferability of quotas is an essential feature if a quota system is to increase the economic efficiency in the fishery. Quotas are sold or leased from less efficient vessels to more efficient ones. In the Icelandic system there is a limit to the consolidation of quotas in each species but nevertheless there have been concerns when quotas have been sold or leased from towns or regions where fishing is the mainstay of the economic activity. In order to address such concerns, special regional quotas were introduced in 2002. The authorities set aside a part of the TAC for specific species and distributed it to rural regions. As ITQs are determined as a percentage of TACs, this meant that the regional quotas were distributed at the cost of quota holders. Quota holders were not compensated for their loss. These quotas are a relatively small share of the total TAC and decisions regarding their distribution are taken by the Minister of Fisheries. These decisions are based on various factors, such as the employment status of the town or region concerned, whether quotas have been leased or sold from the area, how dependent the region is upon fisheries, etc. The idea behind the regional quotas is to help the communities rather than the fishing firms directly.

A recent study indicates that the effects of the regional quotas differ widely from one region to another (Karlsson and Johannesson, 2016). Interestingly, the regional quota allocation has also benefitted the greater capital region, due to its geographical proximity to some of the regions that received regional quotas. This is probably due to the importance of the greater capital region in processing and handling of fish (Karlsson and Johannesson, 2016).

Whether and how the ITQ system has affected the regional development in Iceland is a complicated issue as factors other than fisheries have an effect on whether people and businesses leave or enter various regions.[27]

The coastal fisheries system aimed to accommodate new entrants with small vessels, but the efficiency of this system is questionable

Although the small vessel fishery was finally incorporated into the quota system in 2004, demands were still made for specific measures for smaller vessels, mostly on the ground that entry into the fishing industry was difficult for newcomers. Also, small-scale hand-line fishing was considered by some to be ecologically superior to other fishing methods and that encouraging such activities would create employment and revitalize fishing communities.

To meet such demands, the authorities allowed for a specific coastal fishery system, which opened up in 2009. This is mainly a cod-fishery where small vessel owners can apply for a specific license. The only gear allowed is hand-line and the fishing season is limited to the summer months. In very broad terms, the coastal waters are divided into 4 parts (roughly, north-south-east-west). Only fishing vessels with appropriate licenses can fish in the designated area. A share of the total TAC for cod is allotted to the coastal fishery every year and is distributed between the different fishing areas. There are limits to how much each vessel can land in a day and when the total allowable catch for each area is reached, the fishing in that area stops. This fishery is well monitored and, as in all other fisheries, the catches are all weighted at official weights which exist in all ports.

This coastal fishery system rapidly turned into a derby-style fishery, where fishers compete to fish as much as quickly as possible, and the economic efficiency and results on the ease of entry of newcomers is questionable. This fishery is mostly carried out by seasoned fishers that had already left the industry or are still quota holders.[28]

6.4. Lessons learned

Averting a potential crisis threatening an economically vital industry provided the political drive to establish a sustainable resource management system

The introduction of the Icelandic ITQ system for managing its fisheries was a major reform spurred by an imminent collapse of the most important fish stock, which would have put the fishing industry in peril. Given the importance of the fishing activity to the Icelandic economy, people were willing to undertake strong measures. Having positive experience from similar measures on a smaller scale helped. Such a collapse would have meant economic hardship for the country as a whole. The ITQ system provided the correct incentives for the sustainable harvesting of fish and made it possible for fishers to safeguard stocks through decreasing effort and catches, while at the same time securing their long-term economic future. Such fundamental reforms were only possible to implement in such a short time period because of the perceived imminent threat.

Regarding other policy measures available at the time, it had become apparent that traditional measures, such as input controls (e.g. days-at-sea restrictions, gear restrictions) and output controls (TACs) had not been successful in bringing about sustainable extraction levels from the resources while at the same time the economic efficiency was poor. In that sense, the authorities had run out of policy options.

Although some of the design features of the Icelandic ITQ system have been criticised and various changes have been made over time to meet certain economic and political demands, it is still a success measured in economic efficiency and as a way of drastically reducing fishing effort to safeguard the sustainability of the fish stocks. Biodiversity was not one of the main issues when the system was introduced and other direct measures have been used to secure biodiversity in the marine ecosystem. Safeguarding biodiversity can nevertheless be seen as a positive by-product of the fisheries rebuilding process through the use of the ITQ system.

Overall economic gains of the ITQ reform were positive, but it still generated winners and losers, which consequently led to further reforms

Interestingly, the main stakeholders engaged in the reform design and implementation were government authorities, including scientists, rather than fishers or their associations. Introducing a property rights based system, such as ITQs, leads to changes that benefit some more than others, especially when fishing rights are freely transferable. People who live in fishing regions from which quotas are sold or leased are often left with few other employment opportunities and experience economic and social hardships. Although the quota owners receive payment for their quotas, others that depended on the fishing activity for their livelihood, directly or indirectly, do not receive such payments. Therefore, although the general economic outcome of such reforms is positive, there are clearly those that gain and those that lose from such reforms.

Some industry stakeholders, such as fishers and people whose livelihood depended to a great extent on the fishing (such as people in the processing industry and people living in rural areas dependent on fishing) were not explicitly engaged in the reforms and the implementation of the ITQ system. The subsequent amendments of the system to meet demands from different stakeholders such as small-vessel owners, as well as the regional municipalities, raises the question whether their inclusion into the design and implementation phases of the reforms would have led to the introduction of a different system than the one that was eventually adopted. The answer to that question is not simple, and it may be argued that such sweeping reforms would have been difficult to implement as quickly as was the case, if the process had included the participation of all the different stakeholders. Including every possible stakeholder group would have taken time and resulted in a political debate at every step of the process. On the other hand, limited initial stakeholder engagement may have led to piecemeal amendments to the system over time to respond to specific stakeholder demands, which in some instances may have undermined the sustainability and efficiency of the system.

Notes

1. Demersal fish live and feed on or near the bottom of seas or lakes.
2. The Marine Research Institute is a government agency under the auspices of the Ministry of Fisheries that provides the Ministry with scientific advice based on its research on marine resources and the environment.
3. Primarily the United Nations Convention on the Law of the Sea (UNCLOS).
4. Prior to this, fishing in Iceland was in many ways very primitive through the ages and to a large extent seen and organised as a side-activity to farming, which was the mainstay of the economy.
5. This is a very general and simplified overview of the history of fishing and fisheries in Iceland. A more detailed discussion can be found in Arnason (1995) and Arnason and Agnarsson (2003).
6. During the Great War (1914-18) and World War II (1939-45) foreign fleets were almost non-existant on fishing grounds off Iceland.
7. These measures proved to be ineffective in lowering the fishing effort for many reasons. Most importantly, technical advances, such as more powerful engines and more efficient gear, resulted in effort creep which outpaced all the stringencies put in place through regulation. Above all, there was no or little incentive for each fishing firm to reduce its own individual level of effort, representing the well-known problem of free riding and the commons.
8. For a recent survey on attitutes towards the ITQ system by small-boat fishermen, see Chambers and Carothers (2016).
9. These catch rules have been changed slightly over time. For a discussion of catch rules in Iceland, their history and rationale, see Hagfræðistofnun (2007).
10. See e.g. Clark and Munro (1982), Arnason (1991), R.Q. Grafton (1996) and Hannesson (2000).
11. For a discussion see e.g. Danielsson (1994), Arnason (2005), Matthiasson (2008) Asche, Bjorndal and Bjorndal (2014).
12. For a discussion see Schrank (2003).
13. See OECD (2012).
14. If the growth rate of the fish stock in question is higher than the discount rate of fishers, *ceteris paribus*.
15. The notion of the "Tragedy of the Commons" is attributed to Hardin (1968). For empirical studies, see e.g. McWhinnie (2007).
16. OECD (n.d.), "Country Note on National Fisheries Management Systems – Iceland", pp. 21.
17. For a discussion on similar issues in New Zealand, see Mace, Sullivan and Cryer (2014) and for a general discussion of how incentive based measures may be applied to help conserve biodiversity see Pasecoe et al. (2010) and Innes et al. (2015).
18. See Kokorsch (2015) and Chambers and Carothers (2016).

19. See Anderson, Arnason and Libecap (2010).
20. For a survey of different perceptions regarding the fairness and efficiency of the system see Chambers and Carothers (2016).
21. See Haraldsson and Carey (2011) and Matthiasson (2008).
22. This overview is very general. For a more detailed discussion see Matthiasson (2008).
23. See Matthiasson (2008) for more detail on how the tax system operates and background information on the legislative activity that lead up to the its introduction.
24. The fishing year begins 1 September and ends 31 August.
25. Fisheries Directorate.
26. Haraldsson (2008).
27. See Runolfsson (1997) and Ásgeirsson (2012).
28. University Centre of the Westfjords (2010).

References

Agnarsson, S. et al. (2016), "Consolidation and distribution of quota holdings in the Icelandic fisheries", *Marine Policy, http://dx.doi.org/10.1016/j.marpol.2016.04.037.*

Anderson, T. et al. (2010), "Efficiency Advantages of Grandfathering in Rights-Based Fisheries Management", *NBER Working Paper* No. 16519 (November).

Arnason, R. (2005), "Property rights in fisheries: Iceland's experience with ITQs", *Reviews in Fish Biology and Fisheries*, Vol. 15, No. 3, pp. 243-264.

Arnason, R. (1995), *The Icelandic Fisheries The Evolution of a Fishing Industry*, Fishing News Books. Oxford.

Arnason, R. (1993), "The Icelandic individual transferable quota system: a descriptive account", *Marine Resource Economics*, Vol. 8, pp. 201-218.

Arnason, R. (1991), "Efficient management of ocean fisheries", *European Economic Review*, Vol. 35, pp. 408-417.

Arnason, R. and S. Agnarsson (2003), "The role of the fishing industry in the Icelandic economy: A historical examination", *Institute of Economic Studies Working Papers*, W03:08. University of Iceland.

Asche, F. et al. (2014), "Development in fleet fishing capacity in rights based fisheries", *Marine Policy*, Vol. 44 (February), pp. 166-171.

Ásgeirsson, G. (2012), *Kvótakerfið í fiskveiðum. Tilurð þess og áhrif á byggð og samfélag* [The quota system in fisheries: The emergence and influence of communities and community], unpublished BA-thesis, University of Iceland.

Chambers, C. and C. Carothers (2016), "Thirty years after privatization: A survey of Icelandic small-boat fishermen", *Marine Policy* (in press).

Clark, C.W. and G.R. Munro (1982), "The economics of fishing and modern capital theory: A simplified approach", In Mirman, L.J. and D.J. Spulber (eds.), *Essays in the Economics of Renewable Resources*, North-Holland.

Danielsson, A. (1997), "Fisheries management in Iceland", *Ocean and Coastal Management*, Vol. 35, Issues 2-3.

Fjársýsla ríkisins [State Accounts] (2016), *Ríkisreikningur 2015*. [Treasury accounts 2015].

Grafton, R.Q. (1996), "Individual transferable quotas: theory and practice", *Reviews in Fish Biology and Fisheries*, Vol. 6, Issue 1, pp. 5-20.

Hafrannsóknastofnun [MRI] (1975), *Ástand fiskistofna og annarra dýrategunda á Íslandsmiðum og nauðsynlegar friðunaraðgerðir innan íslenskrar fiskveiðilandhelgi*, [State of fish stocks and other species in Icelandic waters and the necessary conservation measures in Icelandic waters], Sérrit Hafrannsóknastofnunar [MRI Special publication], Hafrannsóknastofnun [MRI], Reykjavik.

Hagfræðistofnun [Institute of Economic Studies] (2007), *Þjóðhagsleg áhrif aflareglu* [Macroeconomic effects of HCR], Report No. C07:09, Hagfræðistofnun [Institute of Economic Studies] Háskóla Íslands. Reykjavik.

Hannesson, R. (2000), "A note on ITQs and optimal investment", *Journal of Environmental Economics and Management*, Vol 40, pp. 181-188.

Hardin, G. (1968), "The Tragedy of the Commons", *Science*, 162, pp. 1243-1248.

Haraldsson, G. (2008), "Impact of the Icelandic ITQ system on outsiders", *Aquatic Living Resources*, Vol. 21, pp. 239-245.

Haraldsson, G. and D. Carey (2011), "Ensuring a Sustainable and Efficient Fishery in Iceland", *OECD Economics Department Working Papers*, No. 891. OECD Publishing, Paris, *http://dx.doi.org/10.1787/5kg566jfrpzr-en*.

Innes, J. et al. (2015), "Mitigating undesirable impacts in the marine environment: A review of market-based management measures", *Frontiers in Marine Science*, Vol. 2. Article 76.

Jakobsson, J. (1979), "Um forsendur „Svörtu skýrslunnar“ [The criteria "Black Report"] *Ægir*.

Jóhannesson, G.T. (2004), "How 'cod war' came: The origins of the Anglo-Icelandic fisheries dispute", 1951-61. *Historical Research*, Vol. 77, Issue 198, pp. 543-574.

Karlsson, V. and H. Johannesson (2016), *Skýrsla um ráðstöfun aflamangs sem dregið er frá heildarafla og áhrif þess á byggðafestu* [Report on the TAC and its effects on sustainability], Rannsóknarmiðstöð Háskólans á Akureyri [Research at the University of Akureyri].

Kokorsch, M. et al. (2015), "Improving or overturning the ITQ system? Views of stakeholders in Icelandic Fisheries", *Maritime Studies*, pp. 14-15.

Mace, P.M. et al. (2014), "The evolution of New Zealand's fisheries science and management systems under ITQs", *ICES Journal of Marine Science*, 71(2), pp. 204-215.

Matthiasson, T. (2013), "Closing the open-sea: Development of fishery management in four Icelandic fisheries", *Natural Resources Forum*, Vol. 27, No. 1.

Matthiasson, T. (2008), "Rent Collection, Rent Distribution, and Cost Recovery: An Analysis of Iceland's ITQ Catch Fee Experiment", *Marine Resource Economics*, 23, No. 1 (2008): 105-117.

McWhinnie, S. (2007), "The Tragedy of the Commons in International Fisheries: An Empirical Examination", *The University of Adelaide School of Economics Research Paper*, No. 2007-05.

Ministry for the Environment and Natural Resources (MENR) (2014), *The Fourth National Report to the Convention on Biological Diversity*, Reykjavík, *www.cbd.int/doc/world/is/is-nr-04-en.pdf* (accessed 24 August 2016).

Ministry for the Environment and Natural Resources (MENR) (2010), "Welfare for the Future: Iceland's National Strategy for Sustainable Development – Priorities 2010-13", Ministry for the Environment, Reykjavík.

National Economic Institute [Þjóðhagsstofnu] (1999), *Þróun sjávarútvegs, kvótakerfið, auðlindagjald og almenn hagstjórn* [Development of the fisheries quota system, resource tax and economic management]. Þjóðhagstofnun [National Economic Institute], Reykjavík, *www.atvinnuvegaraduneyti.is/media/2011/Thjodhagstofnunarskyrsla1999.pdf*.

OECD (2014), *OECD Environmental Performance Reviews: Iceland 2014*, OECD Publishing, Paris, *http://dx.doi.org/10.1787/9789264214200-en*.

OECD (n.d.), "Country note on national fisheries management systems – Iceland", *www.oecd.org/iceland/34429527.pdf* (accessed 30 August 2016), p. 21.

Pascoe, S. et al. (2010), "Use of incentive-based management systems to limit bycatch and discarding", *International Review of Environmental and Resource Economics*, Vol. 4(2), pp. 123-161.

Runolfsson, B. Th. (1997), "Regional impact of the individual transferable quotas in Iceland", In Jones, L. and M. Walker (eds.), *Fish or Cut Bait! The Case for Individual Transferable Quotas in the Salmon Fishery of British Columbia*, Fraser Institute, Vancouver, BC.

Schrank, W.E. (2003), *Introducing Fisheries Subsidies*, FAO, Rome.

Statistic Iceland (2016), *www.statice.is/* (accessed 16 August 2016).

Statistics Iceland (2014), "Rekstraryfirlit sjávarútvegs 2008-14" [Operating Fisheries: 2008-14, *http://px.hagstofa.is/pxis/pxweb/is/Atvinnuvegir/Atvinnuvegir__sjavarutvegur__afkomasja/SJA08109.px/table/tableViewLayout1/?rxid=38f8b711-203c-4c5a-85e9-4d08032dc1ce* (accessed 30 August 2016).

Thordardottir, G. (2016), personal correspondence.

University Centre of the Westfjords (2010), *Úttekt á framgangi og áhrifum strandveiðanna sumarið 2009* [Stock of the progress and effects of coastal fishing in summer 2009], University Centre of the Westfjords, Ísafjörður.

ORGANISATION FOR ECONOMIC CO-OPERATION AND DEVELOPMENT

The OECD is a unique forum where governments work together to address the economic, social and environmental challenges of globalisation. The OECD is also at the forefront of efforts to understand and to help governments respond to new developments and concerns, such as corporate governance, the information economy and the challenges of an ageing population. The Organisation provides a setting where governments can compare policy experiences, seek answers to common problems, identify good practice and work to co-ordinate domestic and international policies.

The OECD member countries are: Australia, Austria, Belgium, Canada, Chile, the Czech Republic, Denmark, Estonia, Finland, France, Germany, Greece, Hungary, Iceland, Ireland, Israel, Italy, Japan, Korea, Latvia, Luxembourg, Mexico, the Netherlands, New Zealand, Norway, Poland, Portugal, the Slovak Republic, Slovenia, Spain, Sweden, Switzerland, Turkey, the United Kingdom and the United States. The European Union takes part in the work of the OECD.

OECD Publishing disseminates widely the results of the Organisation's statistics gathering and research on economic, social and environmental issues, as well as the conventions, guidelines and standards agreed by its members.

OECD PUBLISHING, 2, rue André-Pascal, 75775 PARIS CEDEX 16
(97 2017 04 1 P) ISBN 978-92-64-26952-1 – 2017

www.ingramcontent.com/pod-product-compliance
Ingram Content Group UK Ltd.
Pitfield, Milton Keynes, MK11 3LW, UK
UKHW051507290926
15471UKWH00008B/1467

9 789264 269521